LIFE SKILLS 2
AND
TEST PREP

Ronna Magy

Howard Pomann

with Jennifer Gaudet

PEARSON
Longman

Life Skills and Test Prep 2

Pearson Education, 10 Bank Street, White Plains, NY 10606

Acknowledgments: The authors wish to acknowledge with gratitude the following reviewers, who helped shape the content and approach of *Life Skills and Test Prep 2*: Dr. Maria H. Koonce, Broward County Schools, Ft. Lauderdale, FL • Dr. G. Santos, The English Center, Miami, FL • Edith Uber, Santa Clara Adult Education, Santa Clara, CA • Merari L. Weber, Metropolitan Skills Center, Glendale Community College, Los Angeles, CA • Theresa Warren, East Side Union High School District, San Jose, CA.

Special thanks to June Pomann for her editorial input and feedback

Staff credits: The people who made up the *Life Skills and Test Prep 2* team, representing editorial, production, design, and manufacturing, are Maretta Callahan, Tracey Cataldo, Dave Dickey, Christine Edmonds, Irene Frankel, Judy Li, Martha McGaughey, Marcia Schonzeit, and Jane Townsend.

Cover Image: José Ortega c/o theispot.com
Text composition: ElectraGraphics, Inc.
Text font: 11 pt Minion
Illustrations: George Thompson
Technical art: Tinge Design Studio

Library of Congress Cataloging-in-Publication Data
Magy, Ronna.
   Life skills and test prep 2 / Ronna Magy, Howard Pomann, with Jennifer Gaudet.
      p. cm.
   ISBN 0-13-199179-5 (student bk.)
   1. English language—Textbooks for foreign speakers. 2. English language—Examinations—Study guides. 3. Life skills—Problems, exercises, etc. I. Pomann, Howard. II. Gaudet, Jennifer. III. Title.
   PE1128.M3325 2007
   428.2'4—dc22

                                        2006100912

ISBN-13: 978-0-13-199179-8
ISBN-10: 0-13-199179-5

LONGMAN ON THE **WEB**

Longman.com offers online resources for teachers and students. Access our Companion Websites, our online catalog, and our local offices around the world.

Visit us at **longman.com**.

Printed in the United States of America

5 6 7 8 9 10–V004–15 14 13 12 11 10

Contents

Correlations vi

To the Teacher x

To the Student xii

Unit 1: School 1

Lesson 1   School Registration 2

Lesson 2   Answering Personal Information Questions 4

Lesson 3   A Class Schedule 6

Lesson 4   Identifying School Personnel 8

Lesson 5   Home–School Communication: Telephoning 9

Lesson 6   Home–School Communication: Writing a Note 10

Lesson 7   Classroom Communication: Making Requests and Asking for Permission ... 12

Unit 1 Test 14

Unit 2: Family 19

Lesson 1   Identifying Family Members 20

Lesson 2   Giving Information About Family Members 22

Lesson 3   Describing People 23

Lesson 4   Complimenting People 27

Lesson 5   Good News and Bad News 29

Unit 2 Test 30

Unit 3: Talking on the Phone 35

Lesson 1   Calling Someone 36

Lesson 2   Taking a Message 37

Lesson 3   Recorded Messages 40

Lesson 4   Phone Directories I 42

Lesson 5   Phone Directories II 44

Unit 3 Test 46

Unit 4: Community Life 51

Lesson 1   An Events Calendar 52

Lesson 2   Invitations 54

Lesson 3   Giving and Getting Directions 56

Lesson 4   Traffic Signs 60

Lesson 5   At The Post Office I 61

Lesson 6   At The Post Office II 62

Unit 4 Test 64

Unit 5: Food 69

Lesson 1   Containers 70

Lesson 2   Quantities 72

Lesson 3   Food Labels 74

Lesson 4   Comparing Values 77

Lesson 5   A Restaurant Menu 80

Lesson 6   Clarification Strategies 82

Unit 5 Test 84

Unit 6: Money and Shopping 89

Lesson 1   Using an ATM 90

Lesson 2   Reading Receipts 92

Lesson 3   Writing Checks 94

Lesson 4   Shopping 97

Lesson 5   Returning and Exchanging Purchases 98

Unit 6 Test 100

Unit 7: Understanding Measurements 105

Lesson 1   Temperatures in Fahrenheit and Celsius 106

Lesson 2   Measuring Dimensions 108

Lesson 3   Measuring Distance 110

Unit 7 Test 112

Unit 8: Housing 115

Lesson 1   Finding an Apartment for Rent 116

Lesson 2   Renting an Apartment 119

Lesson 3   Housing Problems 120

Unit 8 Test 122

Unit 9: Health 125

Lesson 1 Parts of the Body 126

Lesson 2 Injuries 129

Lesson 3 Feeling Sick 131

Lesson 4 Making an Appointment 133

Lesson 5 Medical History Forms 134

Lesson 6 Medicine 137

Lesson 7 Medicine Labels 139

Unit 9 Test 142

Unit 10: Safety Procedures 147

Lesson 1 Safety Warnings 148

Lesson 2 Calling 911 153

Lesson 3 Communicating with Police 155

Unit 10 Test 156

Unit 11: Getting a Job 161

Lesson 1 Help Wanted Ads 162

Lesson 2 Job Application I 165

Lesson 3 Job Application II 167

Lesson 4 A Job Interview 169

Unit 11 Test 170

Unit 12: On the Job 173

Lesson 1 Pay Day 174

Lesson 2 An Employee Accident Form 176

Lesson 3 A Work Schedule 178

Lesson 4 Computers 181

Unit 12 Test 182

Map of the World 186

Map of the United States and Canada 188

U.S. and Canadian Postal Abbreviations.. 189

U.S. and Canadian Capitals 189

Audioscript 190

Medical History Form 197

Job Application Form 199

Employee Accident Report Form 201

Test Answer Sheets for Units 1–12 203

Correlations

Unit 1: School and the Classroom	CASAS*	LAUSD**	Florida***
Lesson 1: School Registration	0.2.1, 0.2.2, 2.5.5	1, 5, 6, 62	3.05.01, 3.14.02
Lesson 2: Answering Personal Information Questions	0.2.1, 0.2.2, 2.5.5	5	3.05.01, 3.14.02
Lesson 3: A Class Schedule	0.1.2, 0.1.6, 1.1.3, 2.3.2	14	3.8.03, 3.14.02, 3.15.08
Lesson 4: Identifying School Personnel	0.1.2, 4.1.8	12	3.01.01
Lesson 5: Home–School Communication: Telephoning	0.1.2, 0.1.4, 2.1.8	16a, 10a	3.06.02, 3.06.04, 3.14.04
Lesson 6: Home–School Communication: Writing a Note	0.1.2, 0.2.3, 2.5.5	16b	3.14.04, 3.15.12
Lesson 7: Classroom Communication: Making Requests and Asking for Permission	0.1.2, 0.1.3	8	3.05.03, 3.15.01
Unit 2: Family	**CASAS**	**LAUSD**	**Florida**
Lesson 1: Identifying Family Members	0.1.2	4	3.14.01
Lesson 2: Giving Information About Family Members	0.1.2, 0.2.1	4	3.05.01, 3.14.01, 3.15.01
Lesson 3: Describing People	0.1.2	3, 63	3.05.01, 3.15.01
Lesson 4: Complimenting People	0.1.4	10c	3.05.03
Lesson 5: Good News and Bad News	0.1.2, 0.1.4	10b	3.05.03

*CASAS: Comprehensive Adult Student Assessment System
**LAUSD: Los Angeles Unified School District (ESL Beginning High content standards)
***Florida: Adult ESOL High Beginning Standardized Syllabi

Unit 3: Talking on the Phone	CASAS	LAUSD	Florida
Lesson 1: Calling Someone	2.1.8, 4.5.4	17	3.04.01, 3.06.02
Lesson 2: Taking a Message	0.1.6, 2.1.7, 4.5.4	21	3.04.01, 3.06.02
Lesson 3: Recorded Messages	2.1.7, 2.5.6, 4.5.4	18	3.04.01, 3.06.02
Lesson 4: Phone Directories I	2.1.1	19, 58	3.06.05
Lesson 5: Phone Directories II	2.1.1	19, 58	3.12.01, 3.06.05
Unit 4: Community Life	CASAS	LAUSD	Florida
Lesson 1: An Events Calendar	2.3.2, 2.61, 2.62	22, 25	3.08.01, 3.08.03, 3.12.01, 3.14.02
Lesson 2: Invitations	0.2.3, 0.2.4, 2.6.1, 2.6.3	9	3.05.03
Lesson 3: Giving and Getting Directions	0.1.2, 0.1.4, 1.1.3, 1.9.4, 2.2.1, 2.2.5	23	3.09.03, 3.12.01
Lesson 4: Traffic Signs	1.9.1, 2.2.2	41	3.09.04
Lesson 5: At the Post Office I	2.4.2	24a	3.12.01, 3.12.02
Lesson 6: At the Post Office II	2.4.3, 2.5.4	24b, 24c	3.08.02, 3.12.01, 3.12.02, 3.15.08
Unit 5: Food	CASAS	LAUSD	Florida
Lesson 1: Containers	1.1.7, 1.38	34	3.11.01
Lesson 2: Quantities	1.1.7, 1.38	31	3.11.01
Lesson 3: Food Labels	1.2.1, 1.38 1.6.1, 3.5.1, 3.5.2	35	3.7.05, 3.11.01
Lesson 4: Comparing Values	1.2.2, 1.2.4, 1.38	32	3.11.01, 3.11.03
Lesson 5: A Restaurant Menu	1.38, 2.6.4	36, 62	3.11.01, 3.12.03
Lesson 6: Clarification Strategies	0.1.6	36, 11	3.15.01

Unit 6: Money and Shopping	CASAS	LAUSD	Florida
Lesson 1: Using an ATM	1.8.1	29, 59	3.08.06
Lesson 2: Reading Receipts	1.2.3, 1.3.5, 1.6.4, 5.4.2, 6.0.2, 6.1.2, 6.1.3, 6.1.4, 6.4.1	27	3.08.05, 3.08.06, 3.11.03
Lesson 3: Writing Checks	1.16, 1.8.2	28	3.08.05, 3.08.06
Lesson 4: Shopping	1.1.9, 1.3.7	30	3.11.02
Lesson 5: Returning and Exchanging Purchases	1.3.3	33	3.08.06
Unit 7: Understanding Measurements	CASAS	LAUSD	Florida
Lesson 1: Temperatures in Fahrenheit and Celsius	1.1.5, 2.3.3, 6.6.4	26	3.13.01
Lesson 2: Measuring Dimensions	1.1.4, 6.6.1, 6.6.2	31b	
Lesson 3: Measuring Distance	1.1.3, 1.9.3, 1.9.4, 2.2.5	31b	3.09.03
Unit 8: Housing	CASAS	LAUSD	Florida
Lesson 1: Finding an Apartment for Rent	1.4.1, 1.4.2	37, 38	3.11.04, 3.11.05
Lesson 2: Renting an Apartment	1.4.1, 1.4.2	38	3.11.04
Lesson 3: Housing Problems	1.4.5, 1.4.7, 8.2.6	39	
Unit 9: Health	CASAS	LAUSD	Florida
Lesson 1: Parts of the Body	3.1.1	43	3.07.01
Lesson 2: Injuries	3.1.1		3.07.01, 3.07.02, 3.07.03
Lesson 3: Feeling Sick	3.1.1	45a	3.07.01, 3.07.02, 3.07.03,
Lesson 4: Making an Appointment	3.1.2, 3.1.3	44	3.07.01, 3.07.02, 3.07.03
Lesson 5: Medical History Forms	3.2.1, 3.2.2	45b	3.07.01, 3.07.02, 3.07.03
Lesson 6: Medicine	3.3.1	46	3.07.04
Lesson 7: Medicine Labels	3.3.2, 3.4.1	47	3.07.04

Unit 10: Safety Procedures	CASAS	LAUSD	Florida
Lesson 1: Safety Warnings	3.4.1, 3.4.2	49	3.10.02
Lesson 2: Calling 911	2.1.2, 2.5.1, 5.3.7, 5.3.8	20	3.06.01, 3.10.01
Lesson 3: Communicating with Police	0.1.2, 5.35	42	3.09.05
Unit 11: Getting a Job	CASAS	LAUSD	Florida
Lesson 1: Help Wanted Ads	4.1.3, 4.1.6	51	3.01.01, 3.01.02
Lesson 2: Job Application I	4.1.2, 4.1.6	52	3.01.02, 3.01.03
Lesson 3: Job Application II	4.1.2, 4.1.6	52, 59	3.01.02, 3.01.03
Lesson 4: A Job Interview	4.1.5, 4.1.7, 4.1.8	53, 54	3.02.06
Unit 12: On the Job	CASAS	LAUSD	Florida
Lesson 1: Pay Day	4.2.1, 6.1.1, 6.1.4	56, 62	3.01.05, 3.02.04
Lesson 2: An Employee Accident Form	4.3.4	57, 59a	3.02.01
Lesson 3: A Work Schedule	4.1.6, 4.2.1, 4.2.4, 4.4.3	55b	3.02.01, 3.08.02, 3.15.08
Lesson 4: Computers	4.5.1, 4.5.4	60	3.04.01

To the Teacher

Course Overview

Life Skills and Test Prep 2 is a competency-based, four-skills course for adult ESL students at the high-beginning level. It is designed to help students acquire the language and life skills competencies they need in all their roles—at home, at work, in school, and in their communities. The course also includes listening and reading tests to give students invaluable practice in taking standardized tests, motivating them to achieve their benchmarks and persist in their learning goals.

Unit Organization

There are twelve units, organized thematically. Each unit contains from three to seven lessons, each one focusing on a specific competency, such as reading an ad for an apartment, describing people, completing a job application, or taking a phone message. The first page of the unit lists the lessons in the unit, along with the goal for each lesson.

At the end of each unit, there is a unit test with both a listening and a reading section. This unit test is a multiple-choice test, much like the CASAS test or other standardized tests. Students must bubble in their answers on a separate answer sheet, found in the back of the book. The answer sheet is perforated so students can easily remove it.

Lesson Organization

Lessons are composed of the following elements as appropriate for the competency being presented:

- Learn
- Practice
- Make It Yours
- Listen
- Note
- Bonus

1 *Note:* Listening activities occur throughout the lesson. The icon before the direction line indicates the CD number and track.

Learn

Each lesson begins with a section called Learn, where the target competency is introduced. Some competencies focus on speaking and listening, while others focus on reading and writing. However, all four skills are integrated within the lesson.

Practice

In the Practice section, students apply what they have just learned. Practice exercises vary in type, depending on the competency. Practice sections often present model conversations, such as someone calling about renting an apartment. Here are the steps for most model conversations:

1. Students first listen to the conversation.
2. They listen and repeat.
3. They practice the conversation in pairs.
4. They reverse roles and practice the conversation again.
5. They practice the conversation again, substituting other information provided.

Make It Yours

This section allows students to personalize the material. These activities range from controlled role plays to more open-ended discussions.

Note: In some activities, students may wish to use made-up information to protect their privacy.

Listen

In addition to the listening exercises built into the other sections of the lesson, every unit includes at least one Listen section that focuses on listening discrimination. The Listen section further reinforces the material in the lesson.

Note

Notes on language and culture appear in the lesson as needed. Additional notes give practical information related to the life skill competency. For example, a note in a lesson about using a phone book explains the difference between the White, Yellow, and Blue pages.

Bonus

The Bonus section that occurs at the end of lessons presents optional activities that go beyond the competency, giving students additional speaking and writing practice.

Unit Tests

Unit tests appear after every unit and contain both a listening and a reading section.

Listening

The listening section includes a variety of item types and is divided into two parts: Listening I and Listening II. Below are the five different sets of directions that are on the listening tests.

- Look at the pictures and listen. What is the correct answer: A, B, or C?

- Listen to the sentence. Which of the following means the same as the sentence you heard: A, B, or C?

- Listen to the first part of the conversation. What should the person say next: A, B, or C?

- You will hear a conversation. Then you will hear a question about the conversation. What is the correct answer: A, B, or C?

- Listen. Everything is on the audio CD. Listen to the question and three answers. What is the correct answer: A, B, or C?

Each question in the listening sections is on a separate track on the audio CD. We recommend that you *play each track twice*, pausing for 10 to 20 seconds between each play. This will approximate how listening is presented on standardized tests.

Reading

The reading section tests students' ability to read and answer questions about a variety of print material, such as signs, forms, schedules, and paragraphs.

Answer Sheets

Each unit test is formatted like a standardized test. Students fill in (bubble in) their answers on the perforated answer sheets included in the back of the book. The answer sheets are printed on both sides of the page in case you want the students to take a test twice or to have additional practice completing the required personal information.

Answer Keys

The answer keys and audioscripts for the tests are found in the *Life Skills and Test Prep 2 Teacher's Manual*. Each answer key can be used as a scoring mask to make tests easy to grade. It also serves as a diagnostic tool; each test item is labeled with its corresponding objective, giving you a clear picture of which competencies the student has not yet acquired.

Life Skills and Test Prep 2 Teacher's Manual

In addition to the answer keys described above, the *Life Skills and Test Prep 2 Teacher's Manual* includes a section to prepare students for the tests in the book and for standardized tests. It helps students use an answer sheet, understand the directions in a test, and learn important test-taking strategies. We recommend that you go through this section of the manual with students before they take the Unit 1 Test or before they take the post-test on a standardized test.

The manual also includes a Classroom Methodology section, with general information for using the *Life Skills and Test Prep 2* material. This section suggests ways for doing pair and group work activities, presenting vocabulary, checking answers, and correcting students' language production.

Please ask your Pearson Longman rep about this manual if you do not already have it.

Built-in Flexibility

Life Skills and Test Prep 2 provides 80 to 100 hours of class instruction. All the material in is aimed at high-beginning students. As such, the lessons do not have to be taught in a specific order, and lessons may be skipped. If you do not want to use all the lessons, here are some ideas for how to select which ones to use:

- Ask your students which topics they are interested in and teach only those lessons.

- Give the unit test as a pre-test to find out how students perform. Use the diagnostic information in the *Life Skills and Test Prep 2 Teacher's Manual* to guide you to which lessons students need.

- If you are using *Life Skills and Test Prep 2* along with *Center Stage 2*, use the information in the *Center Stage 2 Teacher's Edition* to direct you to specific lessons.

To the Student

Life Skills and Test Prep 2 will help you improve your scores on ESL tests like the CASAS test. It will help you prepare for these tests in several ways:

- You will learn the English skills you need for the test.

- You will learn about tests and test-taking strategies.

- You will take a test after each unit, which will give you practice in taking tests and using answer sheets.

Preparing to Take a Test

Here are some things you can do to prepare for a test.

☐ Get a lot of sleep the night before the test.

☐ Eat a meal or snack before the test.

☐ Bring two sharpened #2 pencils.

☐ Bring a pencil eraser.

☐ Bring a ruler or a blank piece of paper.

☐ Arrive early at the testing room.

☐ Make sure you can easily see and hear the tester.

☐ Turn off your cell phone.

☐ Try to relax and do your best! Good luck!

Unit 1 School

Lesson 1 **School Registration**
- **Fill out a registration form**

Lesson 2 **Answering Personal Information Questions**
- **Ask and answer questions about personal information**

Lesson 3 **A Class Schedule**
- **Read a class schedule**
- **Ask questions with *When* and *Where***

Lesson 4 **Identifying School Personnel**
- **Learn names for school employees**

Lesson 5 **Home–School Communication: Telephoning**
- **Call school to say you're not coming**

Lesson 6 **Home–School Communication: Writing a Note**
- **Write an absence note to your child's teacher**

Lesson 7 **Classroom Communication: Making Requests and Asking for Permission**
- **Use *Could I* and *Could you* to make requests and ask for permission**

Learn

7 Silvia is registering for school. Look at the registration form. Listen and point. Listen and repeat.

REGISTRATION FORM

Ramos	Silvia	May 17, 2007
Last Name	First Name	Date
5612 West Third Street	Los Angeles	CA	90036
Address	City	State	Zip Code
213-555-6932	6-20-56	Mexico
Phone Number	Date of Birth	Place of Birth

Silvia Ramos

Signature

Practice

PAIRS. Look at the registration form. Student A, ask Student B a question. Student B, answer. Take turns.

> **Example:**
>
> A: *What number is* Date of Birth?
> B: *Number 9.*

REGISTRATION FORM

1. Last Name   2. First Name   3. Date

4. Address   5. City   6. State   7. Zip Code

8. Phone Number   9. Date of Birth   10. Place of Birth

11. Signature

Make It Yours

A   Write your information on the form. (It's OK to use made-up information when you fill out the form.)

B   *PAIRS.* Exchange papers. Check your partner's registration form. Is it complete? Is it written clearly?

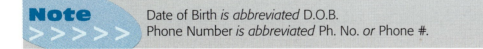

Note
> > > > >   Date of Birth *is abbreviated* D.O.B.
Phone Number *is abbreviated* Ph. No. *or* Phone #.

Learn

A **8** Peter is registering for ESL classes. He is talking to a counselor. Listen to the interview.

A: What's your name?
B: Peter Lee.
A: How do you spell that?
B: P-E-T-E-R L-E-E.
A: What's your address?
B: 640 Alpine Street, Los Angeles, California 90012.
A: What's your phone number?
B: 213-555-6870.
A: What country are you from?
B: I'm from China.
A: What's your date of birth?
B: September 23, 1985.

B Listen to your teacher ask the questions in Exercise A. Repeat the questions.

Practice

A **9** Listen to the interview. Fill in the missing information. Fill in today's date.

ADULT SCHOOL REGISTRATION FORM

Levin   Dimitri
Last Name   First Name   Date

          Elm St.   Teaneck   NJ
Address   City   State   Zip Code

                                        Russia
Phone Number   Date of Birth   Place of Birth

            Dimitri Levin
                    Signature

B *PAIRS.* Check your answers.

Make It Yours

A   *PAIRS.* **Interview your partner. Write your partner's information on the form. (It's OK to use made-up information when you talk to your partner.)**

> **Helpful Expressions**
> ✓ How do you spell that?
> ✓ Could you repeat that?
> ✓ Did you say . . . ?

ADULT SCHOOL   **REGISTRATION FORM**

Last Name   First Name   Date

Address   City   State   Zip Code

Phone Number   Date of Birth   Place of Birth

Signature

B   *PAIRS.* **Check your registration forms. Ask the questions.**

1. Did I spell your name correctly?
2. Is your address correct?
3. Did I spell your street correctly?
4. Is your zip code correct?
5. Are your phone number and date of birth correct?
6. Did I spell your country correctly?

Listen

10   **Listen. What do you hear? Circle *a* or *b*.**

1.   **a.** Steven Jones   **b.** Steven Johnson

2.   **a.** 540 Alpine St.   **b.** 514 Alpine St.

3.   **a.** 212-555-6543   **b.** 212-555-6943

4.   **a.** I'm from Chile.   **b.** I'm from China.

5.   **a.** August 30, 1984   **b.** August 13, 1984

BONUS   *PAIRS.* **Imagine that your partner is a neighbor. He or she wants to register for classes at your school. Tell your partner where to go and what to do.**

Learn

A **11** **Look at the class schedule. Listen and point. Listen and repeat.**

North Valley Adult School CLASS SCHEDULE—NIGHT PROGRAM			
Class	**Evenings**	**Time**	**Room**
ESL 1	M–Th	7:00–9:30 P.M.	9
ESL 2	M–Th	7:00–9:30 P.M.	6
ESL 3	M, W, Th	7:00–9:30 P.M.	4
ESL 4	T, Th	8:00–9:00 P.M.	7
Writing Workshop	M	6:30–8:30 P.M.	10

B   **Look at the class schedule. Match the information.**

_d_ 1. ESL 1	a. meets from 6:30 to 8:30 P.M. on Monday.
____ 2. ESL 2	b. meets in Room 6.
____ 3. ESL 3	c. meets from 8:00 to 9:00 P.M.
____ 4. ESL 4	d. meets in Room 9.
____ 5. Writing Workshop	e. meets Monday, Wednesday, and Thursday.

Note **>>>>>**   *A.M. means in the morning. P.M. can be in the afternoon, in the evening, or at night.*

Practice

 A **12** Listen to the conversations. Listen and repeat.

A: Where does <u>ESL 3</u> meet?
B: In <u>Room 9</u>.

A: When does <u>Computer Literacy</u> meet?
B: Tuesday, from <u>7:00 to 10:00</u>.
A: In the <u>morning</u>?
B: No, in the <u>evening</u>!

West Vista Adult School CLASS SCHEDULE			
Class	**Days**	**Time**	**Room**
ESL 1	M–F	8:00 –10:00 A.M.	8
ESL 2	M, W, F	9:00 –11:00 A.M.	7
ESL 3	T, Th	9:30 –11:30 A.M.	9
Pronunciation	Sa	9:30 A.M. –12:30 P.M.	4
Computer Literacy	T	7:00 –10:00 P.M.	Computer Lab

B *PAIRS.* Practice the conversations with *When* and *Where,* using other classes in the schedule.

Make It Yours

A Fill in your own class schedule.

Class	**Days**	**Time**	**Room**

B *PAIRS.* Compare your schedules. Are they the same?

BONUS What class do you want to take in the future? When does it meet? Look at the schedule of classes for your school.

Learn

 13 Look at the pictures. Listen and point. Listen and repeat.

Renée Dupont

student

Sharon Wong

SHARON WONG PRINCIPAL

principal

Mike Jones

custodian

Robert Yang

ROBERT YANG COUNSELOR

counselor

Steven Cooper

security guard

Bob Rios

teacher

Sonia Gonzalez

receptionist

Practice

PAIRS. Ask about someone's job. Use other jobs and names from Learn. Take turns.

> **Example:**
> A: What does Ms. Dupont do?
> B: She's a student.

Make It Yours

Answer the questions.

1. What is your teacher's name? _____

2. Is there a principal at your school? _____

   If yes, what is the principal's name? _____

   If no, what's the name of the director of the school? _____

3. What other people work at your school? Write their job titles. Ask your teacher for help. _____

   _____

Learn

 14 Listen to the conversation. Listen and repeat.

A: Wading River Adult School. May I help you?
B: This is Lucy Sanchez. I'm in ESL 2.
A: Yes?
B: I'm sorry, but I can't come to class today. <u>I'm sick.</u>
A: I'm sorry. Who's your teacher?
B: Mr. Johnson.
A: And your name again, please?
B: Lucy Sanchez.
A: Thank you.

Practice

PAIRS. **Practice the conversation. Then practice with the information in the box.**

I have to work.	My child is sick.	My car isn't working.

Make It Yours

ROLE PLAY. **Student A, you are the receptionist at your school. Student B, call. You're not coming today. Give a reason.**

 *In the United States, adult students often use their teachers' first names: Bob or Mary. Children use their teachers' last names with Mr., Mrs., Miss, or Ms.: Mr. Barnes or Ms. Green.*

Home–School Communication: Writing a Note

Learn

Read the note. Answer the questions.

> May 10, 2007
>
> Dear Ms. Sato,
>
> My son, Alberto Morales, was absent from school last week because he was sick. He is feeling better today. Please allow him to return to class.
>
> Sincerely,
>
> Sonia Morales

1 Who is the teacher? _____

2. Who is the student? _____

3. Who is the mother? _____

4. Is Alberto a child or an adult? _____

5. Was he in school last week? _____

6. Is he in school today? _____

Practice

Match the parts of the sentences.

__b__ 1. My daughter was sick _____   a. to return to school.

____ 2. Please allow her _____   b. yesterday.

____ 3. She is feeling _____   c. because she was sick.

____ 4. My daughter was absent yesterday _____   d. better today.

Make It Yours

A Write a note to your child's teacher. Explain why your son or daughter was absent from school. Use your imagination.

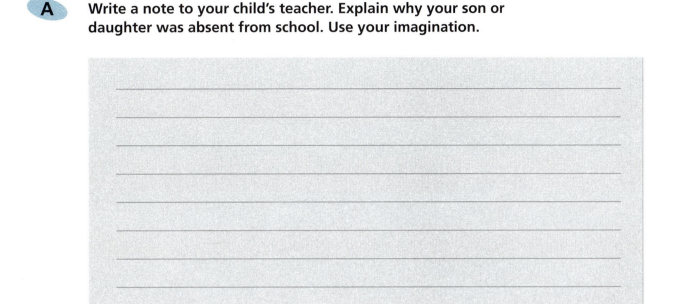

B *PAIRS.* Exchange papers with your partner. Check your partner's note to the teacher.

Does it have a date?

Does it have a signature?

Does each sentence have a capital letter at the beginning and a period at the end?

Does the note start with *Dear* and end with *Sincerely*?

BONUS *TEAMS.* You have 5 minutes. List some other reasons people miss school or work. Share your list with your classmates.

Learn

A   15 **Listen and point to the person who is talking. Listen and repeat.**

Leo: Could I speak to you after class?
Jin: Could I borrow your pen? Thanks.

B **Answer the questions.**

1. Which student is making a request? _____

2. Which student is asking for permission? _____

Practice

A *PAIRS.* **Practice the conversation. Use the words in the box.**

A: Could you <u>give me</u> <u>a piece of paper</u>, please?
B: Sure.

give me	a pen
pass me	a piece of paper

B *PAIRS.* **Practice the conversation. Use the words in the box.**

A: Could I <u>borrow</u> <u>your pen</u>, please?
B: Sure.

borrow	your eraser
use	your pen

C   *PAIRS.* **Practice the conversation. Use the words in the box.**

A: Could I <u>leave early today</u>?
B: Sure.

ask you a question
get a drink of water
leave early today

Make It Yours

A   *PAIRS.* **Read each situation. Make two sentences, one with *Could I* and one with *Could you*.**

1. You forgot your pen.

    1. <u>Could I borrow a pen?</u>

    2. <u>Could you give me a pen?</u>

2. It's noisy in the hall.

    1. _____ the door?

    2. _____ the door?

3. It's cold in the room.

    1. _____ the window?

    2. _____ the window?

4. It's hot in the room.

    1. _____ the window?

    2. _____ the window?

B   *PAIRS.* **Role-play the situations in Exercise A.**

Note
> > > > >

Sometimes we say May I *to ask for permission to do something.* May I *is more formal than* Could I.

Example:
May I talk to you?

BONUS   **Think of another situation like the situations in Exercise A. Create a role play. Present it to the class.**

Unit 1 Test

Before you take the test

(A)(B)(C)(D) Use the answer sheet for Unit 1 on page 203.

1. Print your name.
2. Print your teacher's name.
3. Write your student identification number, and bubble in the information below the boxes.
4. Write the test date and bubble in the information.
5. Write your class number and bubble in the information.

Listening I [Tracks 16–19]

Look at the pictures and listen. What is the correct answer: A, B, or C?

1.

| A | B | C |

2.

| A | B | C |

3.

| A | B | C |

Listening II [Tracks 20–24]

Listen. Everything is on the audio CD.

Reading

Read. What is the correct answer: A, B, C, or D?

SOUTH COUNTY ADULT SCHOOL		
REGISTRATION FORM		

1 Garcia   Juan   September 5, 2007
Last Name   First Name   Date

2 221 Granvia Street   Santa Ana   CA   92704
Address   City   State   Zip Code

3 714-555-0001   2/16/82   Mexico
Phone Number   Date of Birth   Place of Birth

4   Juan Garcia
                   Signature

---

8. On which line is Juan's signature?

    A. line 1

    B. line 2

    C. line 3

    D. line 4

9. What is Juan's phone number?

    A. 2/16/82

    B. September 5, 2007

    C. 92704

    D. 714-555-0001

Centennial Adult School CLASS SCHEDULE			
Class	**Day(s)**	**Time**	**Room**
ESL 1	M, T	6:00–8:00 P.M.	D-106
ESL 2	W, Th	8:00–10:00 P.M.	A-111
ESL 3	F	9:00–11:00 A.M.	D-106

10. Where does ESL 1 meet?

    A. Room D-106

    B. 6:00–8:00 P.M.

    C. Room A-111

    D. on Monday and Tuesday

11. When does ESL 3 meet?

    A. Room D-106

    B. Wednesday and Thursday

    C. on Friday

    D. 8:00–10:00 A.M.

Miss Lee works in the school office at Washington School. She sits at the front desk. She answers the phone and takes messages. Miss Lee also talks to students when they come into the office. Miss Lee likes her job and is friendly to everyone.

Amina came to the United States from Ethiopia a year ago. She is learning English for the first time. She is afraid to speak, but she knows that it is important to try. This morning, Amina went to the school office to practice speaking English with Miss Lee. She asked if she could borrow a pencil. Miss Lee gave Amina a pencil. Then they talked about Amina's new life in the United States. When Amina left to go to her class, she felt very happy about her English.

12. Who is Miss Lee?

    A. She's a custodian.

    B. She's a security guard.

    C. She's a student.

    D. She's a receptionist.

13. Where did Amina talk to Miss Lee?

    A. in the classroom

    B. in the office

    C. with a pencil

    D. on the telephone

1 June 13, 2007

2 Dear Mr. Keith,

3 My daughter, Nancy Nguyen, was absent from school yesterday because she was sick. She is better today.

4 Thank you,

5 Mary Nguyen

14. Who is the student?

  A. Mary Nguyen

  B. in school

  C. Nancy Nguyen

  D. tomorrow

15. Who is the letter from?

  A. Mary Nguyen

  B. Nancy Nguyen

  C. June 13, 2007

  D. Mr. Keith

Unit 2 Family

Lesson 1 **Identifying Family Members**
- Learn words for family relationships

Lesson 2 **Giving Information About Family Members**
- Give basic information about family members

Lesson 3 **Describing People**
- Describe physical characteristics of family and friends
- Use pronouns

Lesson 4 **Complimenting People**
- Give and receive compliments

Lesson 5 **Good News and Bad News**
- Give and receive sympathy and congratulations

Learn

A CD1 TRACK 25 Look at the family tree. Find Yolanda. Listen and point. Listen and repeat.

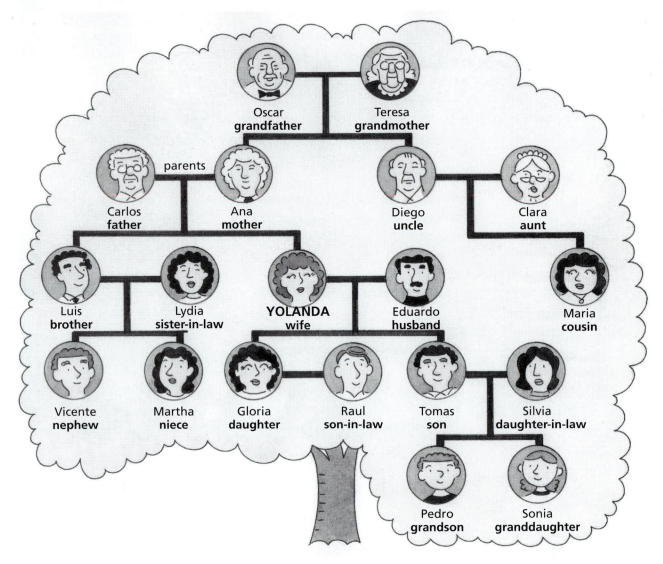

B *PAIRS.* Student A, say a sentence about people in Yolanda's family. Use *He's, She's,* and *They're.* Student B, point to the picture of the person. Take turns.

Examples:

A: *She's Yolanda's daughter.*   B: *They're Yolanda's parents.*
B: *[Point to Gloria.]*   A: *[Point to Carlos and Ana.]*

Practice

Josh _____

Bill _____

Debbie __1__

Alan

Nancy

Phil __2__

Laura _____

Kathy _____ Sarah

A Listen to the descriptions of people in Alan's family. Number the person or people in the order you hear them.

B **PAIRS.** Check your answers. Use names.

> **Example:**
>
> A: Number 1. Debbie is Alan's daughter.
> B: That's right. Number 2. Phil is Alan's son.

C **TEAMS OF 3.** Look at the picture of Alan's family. You have 5 minutes. Write sentences about the people in the picture. Use as many family words as you can. Which team has the most sentences?

> **Examples:**
>
> 1. Nancy is Alan's wife.
> 2. Nancy is Laura's mother-in-law.

BONUS Fill in the blanks.

1. mother and father = _____ parents _____

2. son and daughter = _____

3. grandson and granddaughter = _____

Learn

> **Note** >>>>>> When people in English-speaking countries meet for the first time, they often talk about where they live and work, or where people in their families live and work.

A **27** **Listen to the conversation. Listen and repeat.**

A: Who's this?
B: That's my friend <u>Carol</u>. <u>She</u> lives in <u>Miami</u>. <u>She's married and has two children.</u>
A: What does <u>she</u> do?
B: <u>She works in a bank. She's a bank officer.</u>

B *PAIRS.* **Practice the conversation.**

Practice

PAIRS. **Practice the conversation. Talk about these pictures. Take turns.**

Mary	John	Lew	Barbara

Los Angeles / married, 3 children / an office, a receptionist	Dallas / married, 1 child / a store, a manager	Philadelphia / single / a high school, a teacher	Boston / divorced, 2 children / a hotel, a desk clerk

Make It Yours

You have 5 minutes. Write as many sentences as you can about your friends or family members.

> *Example:*
>
> *My parents live in Tampa. They're retired. My brother Ivan . . .*

_____

_____

_____

Learn

 28 **Look at the pictures. Listen and point. Listen and repeat.**

Height

She's tall.   She's average height.   She's short.

Weight

She's thin.   She's average weight.   She's a little heavy.   She's heavy.

Hair

She has short, curly hair.   She has long, wavy hair.   She has long, straight hair.   He's bald.

Other

He has glasses.   He has a mustache.   He has a beard.   He has freckles.

Practice

A *PAIRS.* **Look at the picture. Student A, describe a person. Student B, point to the person and say the name. Take turns.**

A: She's tall and thin. She has long, curly hair.
B: That's Alice. [*Point to Alice.*]

B  **29** **Listen to the conversation. Listen and repeat.**

A: What does <u>Alice</u> look like?
B: <u>She's tall and thin. She has long, curly hair.</u>

C *PAIRS.* **Practice the conversation. Talk about other people at the picnic.**

D *PAIRS.* **Look at the picture. You have 5 minutes. Together, write as many physical descriptions as you can of the people at the picnic.**

> *Examples:*
> *Monica is short. Ming and Ana are average height.*

_____ is _____ .

_____ are _____ .

_____ has _____ .

_____ have _____ .

E In this paragraph, the pronouns *she, he,* and *they* are underlined. Read the paragraph. Who does each pronoun refer to? Write the names of the people in the blanks.

Marie and her sister Colette are from Haiti. <u>They</u> are good friends, but
_{1.}
<u>they</u> are very different. Marie is average height and average weight. <u>She</u> has
_{2.} _{3.}
short black hair. Her sister is tall and thin. <u>She</u> has long hair. Marie lives in a
_{4.}
large city. <u>She</u> is single and works in a department store. Marie is a sales clerk,
_{5.}
but <u>she</u> wants to be a manager. Colette is married and has two children. <u>She</u>
_{6.} _{7.}
works full time in an office, and her husband Marc is an assembler. <u>He</u> works
_{8.}
in a factory. <u>They</u> live in the suburbs. Marie and Colette want to see each
_{9.}
other more, but <u>they</u> live far away from each other.
_{10.}

1. They *Marie and Colette*

2. They _____

3. She _____

4. She _____

5. She _____

6. She _____

7. She _____

8. He _____

9. They _____

10. They _____

Listen

A **30** Look at the pictures of the cousins, Mike, Sam, and Peter. Listen to the sentences. Each sentence describes one of the cousins. Write the first letter of the name that matches the description. Write *M* for Mike, *S* for Sam, or *P* for Peter.

| Mike | Sam | Peter |

1. _P_   7. _____

2. _____   8. _____

3. _____   9. _____

4. _____   10. _____

5. _____   11. _____

6. _____   12. _____

B   *PAIRS.* Check your answers.

Make It Yours

PAIRS. Student A, describe a person you know. Student B, draw the person. Take turns.

Learn

A **31** Listen and point. Listen and repeat.

a. good-looking _____

b. adorable _____

c. cute _____

d. handsome _____

e. pretty _____

f. beautiful _____

g. friendly _____

h. thoughtful _____

i. kind _____

Note **>>>>>** Handsome *is used for men or boys.* Pretty *is used for women or girls.* Adorable *and* cute *are used for babies or children.*

B **32** Listen to the compliments. Number the pictures in the order you hear them.

C *PAIRS.* Check your answers.

D **33** Listen and repeat.

Practice

A *PAIRS.* Practice giving a compliment.

A: What <u>an adorable baby</u>!
B: Thanks!

B *PAIRS.* Student A, choose a picture and give a compliment.
Student B, point to the picture and say *thanks.*

C   *DICTATION.* Write the sentences you hear.

1. _____

2. _____

3. _____

4. _____

5. _____

6. _____

D *PAIRS.* Check your answers.

BONUS What other times do you give compliments? What other
compliments do you know? Tell the class.

Learn

A 35 **Listen to the conversation. Listen and repeat.**

A: My son is getting married!
B: Congratulations!

A: I lost my job.
B: I'm sorry to hear that.

B *PAIRS.* **Practice the conversations.**

> **Note**
> >>>>>
>
> *After you hear bad news, you usually say* I'm sorry *or* I'm so sorry. *After you hear good news, you usually say* Congratulations. *In both situations, you often add a comment or ask a question to show interest.*
>
> **Examples:**
>
> A: We just bought a house.   A: I got a ticket when I was driving home.
> B: Congratulations! Where is it? B: I'm so sorry. What happened?
> A: It's in Garden City.   A: Well, I went through a stop sign.

Practice

PAIRS. **Student A, say a sentence from the box. Student B, give the appropriate response.**

My wife got a new job.	I got a speeding ticket.	I just became a citizen.
I failed my last test.	We bought a house.	I got a parking ticket.

Make It Yours

PAIRS. **Student A, tell good and bad news about your friends or family. Student B, give an appropriate response and add a comment or a question. Take turns. (It's OK to use made-up information.)**

> **Examples:**
>
> A: My sister just had a baby.   A: My grandfather died last week.
> B: Congratulations! Did she have a B: I'm so sorry. Was he sick
>   boy or a girl?   for a long time?

Unit 2 Test

Listening I [Tracks 36–39]

Look at the pictures and listen. What is the correct answer: A, B, or C?

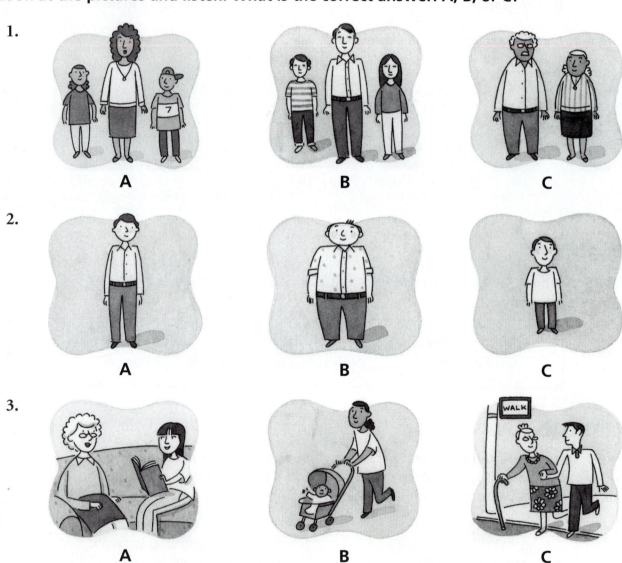

1.

   A   B   C

2.

   A   B   C

3.

   A   B   C

**Listen to the first part of the conversation.
What should the person say next: A, B, or C?**

4. A. It's a pencil.

   B. That's her mother.

   C. That's right.

5. A. Yes, he's at work.

   B. You're very thoughtful.

   C. He's handsome.

6. A. Congratulations!

   B. I'm so sorry.

   C. Thank you!

Reading

Read. What is the correct answer: A, B, C, or D?

Lian and her husband, Shing, are from China. They came to the United States in 1998. They take English classes at night. Shing works at a grocery store. Lian works at a school. Lian and Shing want to save money because they plan to visit their parents and other family members in China.

Lian and Shing have a son named Wei and a daughter named Fan. Wei is tall and thin and likes to read. Fan is short and has long, dark hair. She likes to play the piano.

Wei wants to speak Chinese with his grandparents when his family goes to visit them in China. So every Saturday he studies Chinese. Fan studies Chinese, too, but she is afraid to fly! She wants her grandparents to come to the U.S. to visit. Then she won't have to go on an airplane.

7. Who are Lian and Shing?

    A. Wei and Fan's grandparents

    B. Wei and Fan's children

    C. Wei and Fan's parents

    D. Wei and Fan's teachers

8. What does Wei look like?

    A. He's bald.

    B. He likes to read.

    C. He has black, wavy hair.

    D. He is tall and thin.

9. Who likes to play the piano?

    A. Fan

    B. Lian

    C. Shing

    D. Wei

10. Where do Wei and Fan's grandparents live?

    A. in a school

    B. in China

    C. in the United States

    D. in a store

My Aunt Sol came to the United States eight years ago from the Philippines. She didn't like her job there and was not happy. She came to Denver, Colorado, with her husband, Roger, to study to be a nurse.

In the Philippines, my Uncle Roger worked at the airport as a security guard. He didn't like his job very much either. He also wanted to come to the U.S. to find another career. Now he is studying computer science and wants to find a job.

Now my Aunt Sol is a nurse and likes helping her patients in a hospital near her house. Soon Uncle Roger will get a job as a computer programmer. They are both very happy with their new jobs and in their new country.

11. How long has Aunt Sol lived in Denver?

    A. five years

    B. one year

    C. six years

    D. eight years

12. What does Uncle Roger want to do in his new job?

    A. help patients in a hospital

    B. be a security guard

    C. work with computers

    D. find a new job

STATE HIGHWAY PATROL   00433

Notice to Appear

9/13/07	11:00 A.M.	Thursday
Date	**Time**	**Day of the Week**

David White
Name

111 North Beach Blvd.
Address

Orange Grove
City

Offense: Driving 80 mph in a 60 mph speed zone

---

13. David has some bad news for his parents. What is it?

    A. He lost his job.

    B. He got a parking ticket.

    C. He got a speeding ticket.

    D. He failed his English test.

14. What time does he have to go to court?

    A. at 11 A.M.

    B. on September 13

    C. on Thursday

    D. at 80 mph

Unit 3 Talking on the Phone

Lesson 1   **Calling Someone**
- Begin and end telephone conversations

Lesson 2   **Taking a Message**
- Take a phone message

Lesson 3   **Recorded Messages**
- Respond to phone menu instructions

Lesson 4   **Phone Directories I**
- Read and use the White Pages of a phone directory

Lesson 5   **Phone Directories II**
- Read and use the Yellow, Blue, and White Pages of a phone directory

Learn

 44 A woman is calling an appliance company. Listen to the conversation. Listen and repeat.

Receptionist: Acme Appliance. May I help you?

Caller: This is Dolores Jacobs. May I speak with Mr. Miller?

Receptionist: Let me see if he's here. Please hold.

*   *   *   *   *   *

Receptionist: I'm sorry, he's not available. Can I give you his voice mail?

Caller: Sure, thanks.

Practice

Cover the conversation in Learn. Complete the conversation below with the correct words and your name. You may need capital letters.

available	~~help~~	hold	speak	this	voice mail

A: Acme Electronics. May I _____ help _____ you?

B: _____ is _____. May I _____ with Mr. Miller?
                               (name)

A: Let me see if he's here. Please _____.

    I'm sorry, he's not _____. Can I give you his _____?

B: Sure, thanks.

Make It Yours

PAIRS. **Practice the conversation. Use your name. Take turns.**

Learn

A **45** **A customer is calling a plumber. The plumber is not available. Look at the message and listen.**

While You Were Out

Date _____ 3/29 _____

To _____ Sam Hall _____

From _____ Mrs. Brannon _____

Phone _____ 213-555-6129 _____

Message _____ Problem with kitchen sink. _____

_____

Signature _____ Ana _____

B **Look at some of the questions from the conversation in Learn. Match the questions with the responses.**

_d_ 1. May I help you?

_____ 2. May I take a message?

_____ 3. How do you spell that?

_____ 4. What's the problem?

_____ 5. What's your telephone number?

_____ 6. Did you say 213-555-6129?

a. B-R-A-N-N-O-N.

b. 213-555-6129.

c. I have a problem with my kitchen sink.

d. Yes. May I speak with Sam Hall, please?

e. That's correct.

f. Yes. Please tell him to call Mrs. Brannon.

Practice

While You Were Out

Date _____

To _Ben Johnson_____

From _Pat_____

Phone _____

Message _has a problem with_____

_____

Signature ___Dana Mills_____

B **47** **Listen to the conversation. Complete the message. Use today's date.**

While You Were Out

Date _____

To _Mrs. Anderson_____

From _Bob_____

Phone _____

Message _printer_____

_____

Signature ___Tim Rowe_____

Make It Yours

PAIRS. Read the message. Fill in today's date. Write the phone conversation. Present your conversation to the class.

```
┌─────────────────────────────────────────┐
│           While You Were Out             │
│                                          │
│  Date _____   │
│  To _Ben Johnson_____     │
│  From _Alice West_____     │
│  Phone _803-555-2166_____     │
│ ───────────────────────────────────────  │
│                                          │
│  Message _problem with dishwasher____     │
│                                          │
│  _____    │
│                                          │
│  Signature _Dana Mills_____     │
└─────────────────────────────────────────┘
```

A: Ace Plumbing. May I help you? _____

B: May _____

A: He's not _____

B: Yes, please tell him _____

A: _____

B: W - E - S - T. _____

A: And what's the problem? _____

B: _____

A: _____

B: 803-555-2166. _____

A: OK, I'll _____

B: _____

BONUS *PAIRS. ROLE PLAY.* Student A, you are a receptionist at Joe's Plumbing. Student B, you have a problem with your bathtub. Call Joe's Plumbing. Student A, Joe, the plumber, isn't there. Take a message.

Lesson 3 Recorded Messages

Learn

 48 Listen to the recorded message. Check (✓) the place.

_____ a. a telephone company
_____ b. a school
_____ c. a library
_____ d. a store

Practice

 A **49** Listen and fill in the information.

Los Angeles Occupational Center

1. For information about classes, press _____.

2. To leave a message, press _____.

3. For the computer lab, press _____.

4. To speak with a counselor, press _____.

B **50** Listen and fill in the information.

Telephone Communication Company

1. For problems with telephone service, press_____.

2. For questions about billing, press_____.

3. To speak with a customer service representative, press _____.

4. For sales, press _____.

 C **51** Listen and fill in the information.

Millman's Department Store

1. For customer service, press _____.

2. For store location, press _____.

3. For directions to the store, press _____.

4. For store hours, press _____.

Make It Yours

A **52** **Listen and fill in the information.**

George Washington Library

1. The library is located on South Washington Boulevard in _____.

2. Library hours Monday to Thursday are from _____ to _____.

3. Library hours on Friday and Saturday are from _____ to _____.

4. The library is closed on _____.

5. To speak with a librarian, press _____.

B **53** **Listen and fill in the information.**

Hudson Medical Associates

1. Open Monday to Friday from _____ to _____.

2. To make an appointment, _____ during regular business hours.

3. In case of a medical emergency, press _____.

BONUS

A Write the name of a store. Call the store. Find out its location and hours. Complete the information.

Name of store: _____

Location: _____

Hours: _____

B Write the name of a library. Call the library. Find out its location and hours. Complete the information.

Name of library: _____

Location: _____

Hours: _____

Learn

Look at the White Pages directory from Boston. Answer the questions.

SA Realty Associates 200 Ruggles 02120 617-555-9827

S & K Construction 2925 Washington Av 02119 617-555-6821

Sabatino, Maida 780 Bolyston 02199 617-555-0081

Sackler, Dennis 30 Brattle 02138 617-555-1171

Sage Company 175 Federal 02110 617-555-9338

Sahib, Radoune 32 Calvin 02143 617-555-2451

St. Mary Hospital 1770 Beacon 02445 617-555-0095

1. Which four listings are businesses? _____

   _____

2. Which three listings are people? _____

   _____

3. Why are *SA* and *S & K* listed before *Sabatino*? _____

   _____

4. What does *St.* mean in *St. Mary Hospital*? _____

Practice

A   Complete the information.

1. Name: SA Realty Associates _____

   Address: _____ Street, Boston, MA 02120

   Phone number: _____

2. Name: Maida Sabatino _____

   Address: _____

   Phone number: _____

3. Name: Sage Company _____

   Address: _____

   Phone number: _____

B   *PAIRS.* Check your answers.

Learn

PAIRS. **Look at this section of the White Pages. Answer the questions.**

Clark

George 16 Harcourt 02116	....	617-555-9911
H 95 W Cottage 02125	....	617-555-2082
Harold 35 Greenbush 02130	....	617-555-7655
James Old Colony Rd 02110	....	617-555-9458
Kevin 702 Howland 02125	....	617-555-5241
Kevin 395 Washington 02124	....	617-555-1429

1. What last name do all these people have? _____

2. Why is *H* listed before Harold? _____

3. Why is *Kevin* at *702 Howland* listed before *Kevin* at

   395 Washington? _____

Practice

A **Put the names in the box in alphabetical order.**

Jones	Kim	Kiladze
Ngyuen	Tenzin	Debona

1. _____   4. _____

2. _____   5. _____

3. _____   6. _____

B **Put the names in the box in alphabetical order.**

Milford	Montiero	Miller
Mendez	Mayflower Appliances	Munster

1. _____   4. _____

2. _____   5. _____

3. _____   6. _____

C *PAIRS.* **Check your answers.**

Learn

Look at the directories. Write Blue Pages, White Pages, or Yellow Pages.

1. It lists local town offices. _____

2. It only lists businesses. _____

3. It lists businesses and people. _____

4. It has advertisements. _____

5. It lists U.S. government offices. _____

WHITE PAGES

House Restaurant	174 E 56th	212-555-1127
Insurance Agency	1789 Broadway...	212-555-3538
Marshall, James	606 W 122nd	212-555-0371
John	30 W 61st	212-555-0178
Joyce	1088 Riverside Drive	212-555-2241
K	989 5th Av	212-555-0996
Kathy	209 Av of the Amer	212-555-0371

YELLOW PAGES

Plumbers

All Star Plumbing
52 Medford Way Malden   781-555-9911

Belmont Plumbing
21 Common Avenue Boston   617-555-1327

Jimmy's Plumbing and Heating
See ad this page.
Toll free. Dial "1" & then   877-555-8645

Joe's Plumbing Company
196 Dale Street Waltham   781-555-9611

Plumbing Problems?   No Problem!
Jimmy's here!
• Plumbing
• Heating
• Drain Cleaning
Jimmy's Plumbing and Heating
877-555-8645

BLUE PAGES
Local City and Town Offices

Leeds, Town of

Building Dept
General Information 800-555-5000
Building Inspectors 800-555-5265

Health Dept
General Information 800-555-5000
Public Health 800-555-5266

Police Dept
Emergency only 911
Records 800-555-5262

Traffic and Parking Dept
Parking Ticket Information 800-555-5261
Parking Permit Information 800-555-5261

BLUE PAGES
U.S. Offices

United States Government

Internal Revenue Service
Local Area Office 312-555-9646
24 Hour Recorded Tax Help
Toll Free. Dial "1" & then 800-555-7118

Justice Dept
Community Relations 312-555-4321
Drug Enforcement 312-555-4322

Labor Dept
Occupational Safety and Health 312-555-5326
Worker's Compensation 312-555-5300

Practice

A   Check (✓) the best way to find the information. You may check more than one answer.

Where do you find the phone number of . . .	Blue Pages	Yellow Pages	White Pages
1. a friend?			
2. U.S. Citizenship and Immigration Service?			
3. your local post office?			
4. a plumber?			
5. a classmate?			
6. the town Parking and Traffic Department?			
7. a taxi company?			
8. a school?			
9. a doctor?			
10. an appliance store?			

B   *PAIRS.* Check your answers.

BONUS   Choose a phone company, a hospital, and a school. Find them in the phone book and complete the information. Report to the class.

Phone company: _____

Phone number: _____

I found this information in the _____ Pages.

Hospital (name): _____

Phone number: _____

I found this information in the _____ Pages.

School (name): _____

Phone number: _____

I found this information in the _____ Pages.

Unit 3 Test

Listening I [Tracks 54–57]

You will hear a conversation.
Then you will hear a question about the conversation.
What is the correct answer: A, B, or C?

1. A. Monday to Friday from 10 A.M. to 10 P.M.

   B. Monday to Saturday from 8 A.M. to 10 P.M.

   C. seven days a week

2. A. 0

   B. 1

   C. 2

3. A. on 26th Street

   B. next to the mall

   C. on South Main Street

Listening II [Tracks 58–61]

Listen. Everything is on the audio CD.

Reading

Read. What is the correct answer: A, B, C, or D?

While You Were Out

Date _____ 4/13 _____

To _____ Tim Smith _____

From _____ Nancy Brown _____

Phone _____ 211-555-1111 _____

Message _____ Her new washer doesn't work. _____

_____ Please call her. _____

---

7. Who is the message for?

    A. Tim Smith.

    B. Nancy Brown.

    C. Please call her.

    D. 4/13.

8. Why did Nancy call?

    A. To leave a message.

    B. She called 555-1111.

    C. She has a problem with her washer.

    D. She has a new washer.

Welcome to Microword Computers, your favorite computer store. We are located at 202 West Beach Boulevard in the city of Huntington Park. For help with electronics, press 1. For help with computers, press 2. For technical support, press 3. All other calls, press 0 to speak with an operator.

9. What number should you press if you need help with a computer?

    A. 0

    B. 1

    C. 2

    D. 3

10. What number should you press to speak with an operator?

    A. 0

    B. 1

    C. 2

    D. 3

WHITE PAGES

Sanchez, Humberto 170 SW 127th Pl 300-555-3562

Sanchez, Jose & Margo 131 NE 102 Ave 300-555-3728

Sanchez, Jose 915 W 95 Ave 300-555-8282

YELLOW PAGES

Dentists

Sanchez, Tomas, DDS 200 Eastern Ave 505-555-7777

Sato, Suzanne, DDS 345 Western Ave 505-555-4444

Scott, Michael, DDS 665 Northern Ave 505-555-1122

11. Who lives at 915 W. 95th Avenue?

A. Margo Sanchez

B. Jose Sanchez

C. Jose & Margo Sanchez

D. Humberto Sanchez

12. If you need a dentist, who should you call?

A. Tomas Sanchez

B. Humberto Sanchez

C. Margo Sanchez

D. Jose Sanchez

WHITE PAGES

Clark

George 16 Harcourt 02116	....	617-555-9911
H 95 W Cottage 02125	....	617-555-0081
Harold 35 Greenbush 02130	....	617-555-7655
James Old Colony Rd 02110	....	617-555-9338
Kevin 702 Howland 02125	....	617-555-2451
Kevin 395 Washington 02124	....	617-555-0095

13. What kind of information can you get from the White Pages?

    A. phone numbers and addresses

    B. addresses

    C. names

    D. business information

14. Which of the following names are in alphabetical order?

    A. George, Kevin, Harold

    B. Harold, Kevin, George

    C. George, Harold, Kevin

    D. Kevin, George, Harold

Unit 4 Community Life

Lesson 1   **An Events Calendar**
- **Read calendars**

Lesson 2   **Invitations**
- **Extend and respond to invitations**

Lesson 3   **Giving and Getting Directions**
- **Locate places on a map**
- **Ask for and give directions**

Lesson 4   **Traffic Signs**
- **Identify highway and traffic signs**

Lesson 5   **At the Post Office I**
- **Ask and answer questions about mailing a package**

Lesson 6   **At the Post Office II**
- **Read a postal notice and a mailbox pickup schedule**

Learn

Sunday	Monday	Tuesday	Wednesday	Thursday	Friday	Saturday
Eastside Public Library — Calendar of Events					**February**	
1 Closed	2	3 Internet Class 6:00–8:00 P.M.	4 Homework Help Session 3:00–4:30 P.M.	5	6	7 Mystery Book Group 2:00 P.M.
8 Closed	9 Writers' Workshop 7:00 P.M.	10	11 Homework Help Session 3:00–4:30 P.M.	12	13 Children's Story Hour 10:00 A.M.	14 Valentine Poetry Workshop 1:00 P.M.
15 Closed	16 Library Closed for Presidents' Day	17 Internet Class 6:00–8:00 P.M.	18 Homework Help Session 3:00–4:30 P.M.	19 Teen Book Group 7:00 P.M.	20	21
22 Closed	23	24	25 Homework Help Session 3:00–4:30 P.M.	26	27 Children's Story Hour 10:00 A.M.	28

A Read the calendar. Read the statements. Circle *T* for *True* or *F* for *False*. Correct the false statements.

1. The library is closed on Sundays.   (T) F
2. The Internet Class is on the first and fourth Tuesdays of the month.   T F
3. The Children's Story Hour is on the second and third Fridays of the month.   T F
4. The Homework Help Session is on Wednesdays from 3:00 to 4:30 P.M.   T F
5. The Writers' Workshop is on the second Monday of the month.   T F
6. Presidents' Day is on the third Monday of February.   T F
7. The Teen Book Group is on the third Tuesday of the month at 7:00 P.M.   T F

B *PAIRS.* Check your answers.

Practice

A 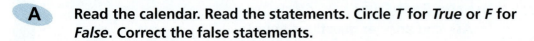 **62** Listen to the conversation. Listen and repeat.

A: When is the <u>Writers' Workshop</u>?
B: It's on the <u>second Monday</u> of the month at <u>7:00 P.M.</u>

B *PAIRS.* Practice the conversation with other information from the calendar in Learn. Take turns.

Make It Yours

A Look at the calendar. Complete the information on the flyers below.

Naples Community Center
October

SUNDAY	MONDAY	TUESDAY	WEDNESDAY	THURSDAY	FRIDAY	SATURDAY
1	2 Exercise for Seniors 10:00–12:00 noon	3 Parent Connection 6:30 P.M.	4	5 Bingo Night 6:00–9:00 P.M.	6 Community Concert 7:30 P.M.	7
8 Children's Story Hour 3:00	9	10	11 Book of the Month Club 7:00 P.M.	12 Bingo Night 6:00–9:00 P.M.	13	14 Teen Connection 6:00–10:00 P.M.
15	16 Exercise for Seniors 10:00–12:00 noon	17 Parent Connection 6:30 P.M.	18	19 Bingo Night 6:00–9:00 P.M.	20	21
22 Children's Story Hour 3:00	23	24	25	26 Bingo Night 6:00–9:00 P.M.	27	28 Teen Connection 6:00–10:00 P.M.
29	30	31 Parent Connection 6:30 P.M.				

1.
Naples Community Center

Children's Story Hour

the _____ and _____
Sunday of each month.

Ages 3 and up.

Bring the family!

550 Marina St.   Naples, CA

2.
Naples Community Center

Exercise for Seniors

Stay fit!
Stay young!

the _____ and _____ Monday
of each month from _____ in
the morning to _____

550 Marina St.   Naples, CA

3.
Naples Community Center

BINGO Night

Come!
Play!
Win!

_____ from
_____ to _____

550 Marina St.   Naples, CA

B *PAIRS.* Check your answers.

BONUS *CLASS.* Bring your public library calendar to class. Discuss the following questions:

Is there a computer class? If yes, when is it?

Is there a story hour for children? If yes, when is it?

Is there a homework help session? If yes, when is it?

Is there a book group? If yes, when is it?

Learn

A Write the words under the pictures.

> go to the park   ~~go to a concert~~   go to a movie
> go to a basketball game   go to a party   go out for coffee

1. _____go to a concert_____

2. _____

3. _____

4. _____

5. _____

6. _____

B  **63** Listen and check your answers. Listen and repeat.

Practice

A   🔘 **64**   **Listen to the conversation. Listen and repeat.**

A: Would you like to <u>go out for lunch</u>?
B: Sure! I'd love to.

B   🔘 **65**   **Listen to the conversation. Listen and repeat.**

A: Would you like to <u>go to a movie</u>?
B: I'm sorry, I can't. I have to work.

Note
> > > > >   *When you say* no *to an invitation, you need to give a reason why you can't go.*

C   *PAIRS.* **Practice the conversations with other activities from Learn.**

Make It Yours

A   **What are some other reasons that people give when they say *no* to an invitation? Write five reasons.**

1. I'm sorry, I can't. I have to _____ pick up my children _____.

2. I'm sorry, I can't. I have to _____.

3. I'm sorry, I can't. I have to _____.

4. I'm sorry, I can't. I have to _____.

5. I'm sorry, I can't. I have to _____.

B   *PAIRS.* **Student A, invite your partner to do something.
Student B, say *yes* or *no*. Take turns.**

BONUS   *PAIRS.* **When you go out with friends, what do you do?
Make a list.**

Learn

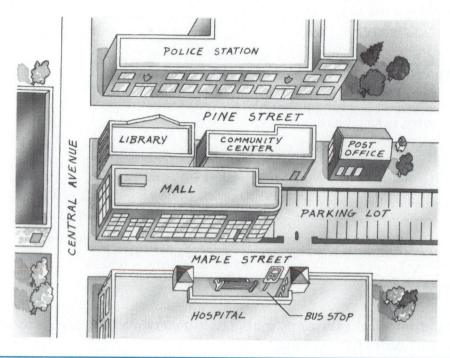

across from	between	in front of	next to	~~on~~	on the corner of

A **Look at the map. Complete the sentences with words from the box.**

1. The police station is _____ on _____ Pine Street.

2. The library is _____ Central Avenue and Pine Street.

3. The community center is _____ the library and the post office.

4. The parking lot is _____ the mall.

5. The hospital is _____ the mall and the parking lot.

6. The bus stop is _____ the hospital.

B 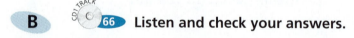 66 **Listen and check your answers.**

Practice

A **Listen to your teacher and repeat.**

A: Where is the <u>bus stop</u>?
B: It's <u>on Maple Street</u>. It's <u>in front of the hospital</u>.

B *PAIRS.* **Practice the conversation. Then ask and answer questions about other places on the map. Take turns.**

Learn

A **67** Listen and point. Listen and repeat.

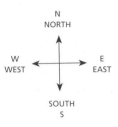

B **68** A visitor is asking for directions. Listen and follow the directions with your finger on the map.

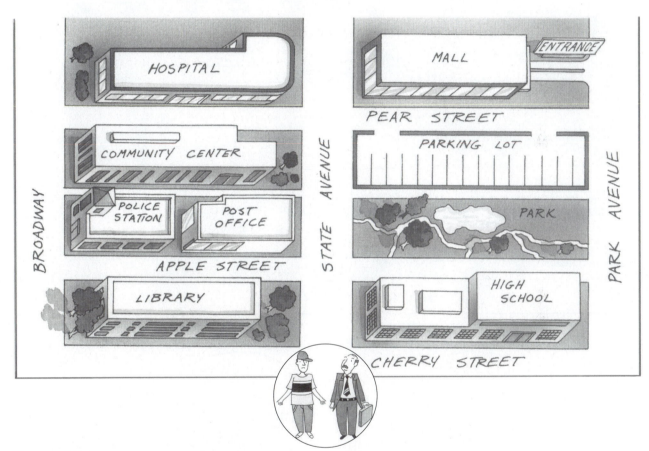

Practice

A **69** Listen to the conversation. Listen and repeat.

A: Excuse me. How do I get to <u>the mall</u>?

B: <u>The mall?</u> <u>Go east for one block.</u> <u>Go left on Park Avenue and go north for three blocks.</u> It's <u>on the left</u>.

A: Thank you.

B *PAIRS.* Practice the conversation. Ask how to get to other places on the map in Learn.

Make It Yours

Read the sentences. Write the names of the places on the map.

1. The **high school** is on Winter Street. It is between the library and the park.
2. The **community center** is on the corner of Spring Street and First Avenue. It is next to the post office.
3. The **parking lot** is on the corner of Spring Street and Second Avenue. It is across from the post office.
4. The **bus stop** is on First Avenue. It's in front of the mall and across from the police station.

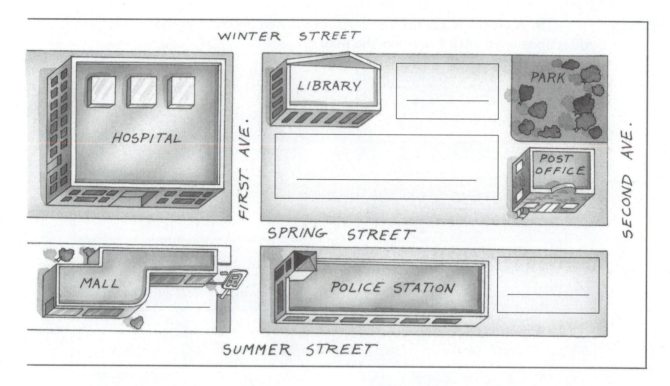

Listen

 70 **Listen. What do you hear? Circle *a*, *b*, or *c*.**

1. **a.** Central Avenue   **b.** Second Avenue   **c.** Central Street
2. **a.** one block   **b.** two blocks   **c.** three blocks
3. **a.** go left   **b.** go right   **c.** on the left
4. **a.** go north   **b.** go west   **c.** go east

BONUS

A Draw a map of the neighborhood around your school. Show your map to another student. Compare maps. Add details.

B *PAIRS.* Ask your partner for directions to places near your school. Take turns.

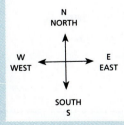

Learn

 71 Look at the traffic signs. Listen and point. Listen and repeat.

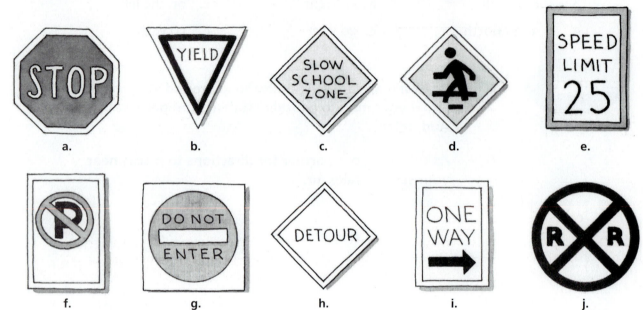

a.   b.   c.   d.   e.

f.   g.   h.   i.   j.

Practice

A Read the sentences. Write the letter of the sign in Learn that matches.

_g_ 1. Do not come in here.

____ 2. Go only in this direction.

____ 3. A train crosses here.

____ 4. People cross the street here.

____ 5. Don't go.

____ 6. Do not park here.

____ 7. Let other cars go first.

____ 8. Street closed. Follow the signs for a different street.

____ 9. School area. Drive carefully.

____ 10. Don't go more than 25 miles an hour.

B PAIRS. Check your answers.

C PAIRS. Student A, choose a traffic sign in Learn. Don't tell Student B. Say a sentence about it. Student B, point to the sign. Take turns.

Example:

A: Let other cars go first.

B: [Points to the yield sign.]

A: That's right.

Learn

A 🔘 72 **Look at the chart. Listen and point. Listen and repeat.**

B 🔘 73 **Listen to the conversation. Listen and repeat.**

United States Postal Service	
Mail Service	**Delivery Time**
Express Mail	Next day
Priority Mail	2–3 days
First-Class Mail	2–3 days
Parcel Post	2–9 days

Customer: How long does <u>Express Mail</u> take?
Clerk: <u>One day.</u>

C *PAIRS.* **Practice the conversation. Ask about different mail services on the chart.**

Practice

A 🔘 74 **Listen to the conversation. Listen and repeat.**

Clerk: May I help you?
Customer: Yes, I want to mail this package to New York.
Clerk: How do you want to send it?
Customer: How long does <u>Parcel Post</u> take?
Clerk: <u>Two to nine days.</u>
Customer: OK. Send it <u>Parcel Post.</u>

B **Cover the conversation in Exercise A. Match the questions with the answers.**

_____ 1. How do you want to send it?   a. Two to three days.

_____ 2. How long does it take?   b. I want to mail this letter to Washington.

_____ 3. May I help you?   c. Priority Mail.

C *PAIRS.* **Check your answers.**

D *PAIRS.* **Practice the conversation in Exercise A with other information from the chart.**

Make It Yours

ROLE PLAY. Student A, you are a customer at the post office. You want to mail a package. Student B, you are a clerk at the post office. Help the customer.

Learn

Read the notice. Complete the sentences.

DELIVERY NOTICE	Today's Date:	Sender's Name:
Sorry we missed you!	3/6/07	Sandra Dean

Item is at:	Available for pick up after:
X Post Office	Date: 3/7/07 Time: 10:00 A.M.
_____	Customer name and address:
____ Letter	Thomas Miller
X Package ____ Other	23 Highland Road, Somerville MA 02144

Delivery Section	Signature:

1. The package is from _____.

2. The package is to _____.

3. The package is at the _____.

4. The customer can pick up the package on _____ after _____.

Learn

Look at the chart. Read the sentences. Circle *T* for *True* or *F* for *False*.

COLLECTION TIMES		
Monday – Friday	**Saturday**	**Sunday**
11:00 A.M.	11:30 A.M.	
1:00 P.M.	1:00 P.M.	**Holiday**
2:30 P.M.	3:30 P.M.	
5:00 P.M.		

1. Mail is picked up at the same time every day of the week.   T (F)

2. Mail is picked up three times on Saturday.   T F

3. Mail is picked up four times on Wednesday.   T F

4. On Tuesday, the last mail pickup is at 2:30 P.M.   T F

5. There are no mail pickups on Sunday.   T F

6. On Friday, the first mail pickup is at 11:00 in the morning.   T F

Practice

A **75** **Listen to the conversation. Listen and repeat.**

Note
>>>>>

ID = identification.
I need to see some ID = Please show me your identification.

Customer:	I'm here to pick up a package. Here's my notice.
Clerk:	I need to see some ID.
Customer:	Here's my driver's license.
Clerk:	Thanks. Just a moment, please. . . . Here it is. Please sign here.

B *PAIRS.* **Practice the conversation.**

C **Read the conversation again. Answer the questions.**

1. What does the customer pick up?

   a. a letter   **b.** a notice   **c.** a package

2. What identification does the customer have?

   a. a notice   **b.** a driver's license   **c.** a package

3. What does the customer sign?

   a. his identification   **b.** his notice   **c.** his package

BONUS   *CLASS.* **A driver's license is one form of government picture identification. What are others? Make a list.**

Unit 4 Test

Before you take the test

Ⓐ Ⓑ Ⓒ Ⓓ | Use the answer sheet for Unit 4 on page 209.

1. Print your name.

2. Print your teacher's name.

3. Write your student identification number, and bubble in the information below the boxes.

4. Write the test date and bubble in the information.

5. Write your class number and bubble in the information.

Listening I [Tracks 76–80]

You will hear a conversation.
Then you will hear a question about the conversation.
What is the correct answer: A, B, or C?

1. A. at the office

    B. on Thursday at 5 P.M.

    C. on Tuesday from 3 to 5 P.M.

2. A. No, he isn't.

    B. Yes, he is.

    C. He's going home.

3. A. near the mall

    B. near the library

    C. across from the supermarket

4. A. in two or three days

    B. $4.05

    C. by next-day mail

Listening II [Tracks 81–84]

Listen. Everything is on the audio CD.

Reading

Read. What is the correct answer: A, B, C, or D?

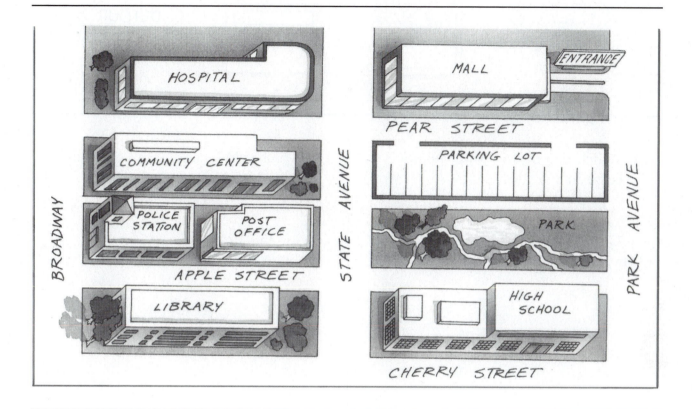

8. Where is the community center?

   A. on Broadway

   B. next to the park

   C. across from the park

   D. across from the hospital

9. What is next to the police station?

   A. the post office

   B. the library

   C. on Broadway

   D. Apple Street

1　　　　**2**　　　　**3**　　　　**4**

10. Which sign means "Stop. Do not come in"?

    A. 1

    B. 2

    C. 3

    D. 4

11. Which sign means "Drive carefully. Schoolchildren near here"?

    A. 1

    B. 2

    C. 3

    D. 4

Mail Type	Delivery Time	Weight of Package	Where To/From?	Price/Delivery
Priority Mail	2-day delivery	1 pound	Zip Codes To: 92692 From: 50636	$4.05 2-day delivery
Express Mail	Next-day delivery	Over 8 ounces up to 2 pounds	Zip Codes To: 92692 From: 50636	$18.80 Next-day delivery

12. How much does Express Mail cost for a 2-pound package?

   A. over 8 ounces

   B. $4.05

   C. next-day delivery

   D. $18.80

13. How long does Priority Mail take?

   A. 1 day

   B. over 8 ounces

   C. 2 days

   D. $4.05

DELIVERY NOTICE	Today's Date:	Sender's Name:
Sorry we missed you!	❶ 3/6/07	❷ Sandra Dean

Item is at:

__X__ Post Office

_____ _____

_____ Letter

__X__ Package   _____ Other

Available for pick up after:

Date: 3/7/07   Time: 10:00 A.M.

Customer name and address:

❸ Thomas Miller

23 Highland Road, Somerville MA 02144

Delivery Section   ❹ Signature:

---

14. On which line should the customer sign his name?

    A. line 1

    B. line 2

    C. line 3

    D. line 4

15. Who should show some ID?

    A. at the post office

    B. Thomas Miller

    C. Sandra Dean

    D. the postal clerk

Unit 5 Food

Lesson 1 **Containers**
- Identify common foods and their containers

Lesson 2 **Quantities**
- Identify and ask for common quantities of foods

Lesson 3 **Food Labels**
- Read basic information on food packaging and labels

Lesson 4 **Comparing Values**
- Read and compare basic information in advertisements

Lesson 5 **A Restaurant Menu**
- Read and order from a menu

Lesson 6 **Clarification Strategies**
- Ask for clarification using different strategies

Learn

A **2** Look at the pictures. Listen and point. Listen and repeat.

1. a bottle of soda

2. a can of tuna fish

3. a box of spaghetti

4. a bag of rice

5. a jar of mayonnaise

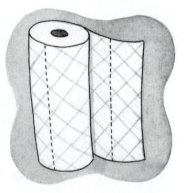

6. a roll of paper towels

7. a container of ice cream

8. a package of cookies

9. a tub of margarine

B   Underline the container words in Learn.

> *Example:*
>
> *a bottle of soda*

Practice

Fill in the blanks. Use the container words in Learn. Use each word once.

1. a ___box___ of cereal

2. a _____ of jelly

3. a _____ of salad dressing

4. a _____ of milk

5. a _____ of muffins

6. a _____ of cream cheese

7. a _____ of toilet paper

8. a _____ of potato chips

9. a _____ of soup

B **3 Listen and check your answers.**

Make It Yours

TEAMS OF 3. **You have 5 minutes. What do we buy in these containers? Make lists. Which team has the most items?**

a can	a bag	a bottle	a box
tomatoes			
a jar	a roll	a package	a container

Learn

> **Note**
> > > > > >
The front labels of some products tell the weight. The weight of an item is in pounds and ounces. The abbreviation for ounce or ounces is oz. The abbreviation for pound or pounds is lb.

A **4** **Listen and point. Listen and repeat.**

four ounces
(a quarter pound)

eight ounces
(a half pound)

twelve ounces
(three-quarters of a pound)

sixteen ounces
(a pound)

twenty-four ounces
(a pound and a half)

thirty-two ounces
(two pounds)

B **Look at the packages in Exercise A. Write the weights in words.**

1. ¼ lb.   =   <u>a quarter pound</u>

2. ½ lb.   =   _____

3. ¾ lb.   =   _____

4. 1 lb.   =   _____

5. 1½ lb. =   _____

6. 2 lb.   =   _____

C *PAIRS.* **How many ounces are in each of these? Ask your partner. Take turns.**

¼ lb.	½ lb.	¾ lb.	1 lb.	1½ lb.	2 lb.

Learn

A   **Look at the pictures. Listen and point. Listen and repeat.**

| 8 oz. | 16 oz. | 32 oz. | 64 oz. | 128 oz. |

B **Fill in the number of cups.**

1 pint	X	X	__2__ cups	16 ounces
1 quart	X	2 pints	_____ cups	32 ounces
½ gallon	2 quarts	4 pints	_____ cups	64 ounces
1 gallon	4 quarts	8 pints	_____ cups	128 ounces

Practice

A **Match the amounts.**

__c__ 1. ½ gallon   a. 32 ounces

_____ 2. 1 quart   b. 8 ounces

_____ 3. 1 cup   c. 2 quarts

_____ 4. 1 gallon   d. 16 ounces

_____ 5. 1 pint   e. 4 quarts

B *PAIRS.* **Check your answers.**

Make It Yours

1. You are making a cake. The recipe asks for 3 cups of milk. You have a pint of milk in your refrigerator. Do you have enough milk? _____

2. Your friend is on a diet and should eat only 4 ounces of meat every day. Should your friend eat a ½-pound hamburger? _____

3. Which is more: ¼ pound of butter, or 6 ounces of butter? _____

Lesson 3   Food Labels

Learn

> **Note**
> **> > > > >**
>
> *Food labels tell the weight of a product or the size of the container. The label also includes the ingredients and the nutrition information. The ingredients are listed in order of the amount contained in the product. The nutrition label lists calories, fat, sodium (salt), and other nutrition facts. Monosodium glutamate (MSG) is a chemical which is often added to food to make it taste better.*

Choice Chicken Soup

Ingredients:
water, chicken broth,
chicken meat, salt

Net Wt. 12 oz.

Lundy's Soup

Chicken
Ingredients:
chicken broth, water, chicken meat,
monosodium glutamate,
salt

Net Wt. 15.5 oz.

Match the description with the label. Write *L* for Lundy's Soup, *C* for Choice Soup, or *L* and *C* for both.

   _L_   1. It has 15.5 oz.

   ____   2. It contains monosodium glutamate.

   ____   3. It contains sodium.

   ____   4. It contains more chicken broth than chicken meat.

   ____   5. It contains more water than chicken broth.

Learn

Look at the nutrition facts on two soup labels. Underline any new words.
Ask your teacher.

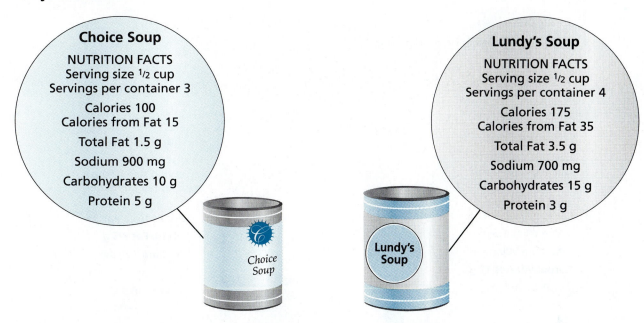

Choice Soup

NUTRITION FACTS
Serving size ½ cup
Servings per container 3

Calories 100
Calories from Fat 15

Total Fat 1.5 g

Sodium 900 mg

Carbohydrates 10 g

Protein 5 g

Choice Soup

Lundy's Soup

Lundy's Soup

NUTRITION FACTS
Serving size ½ cup
Servings per container 4

Calories 175
Calories from Fat 35

Total Fat 3.5 g

Sodium 700 mg

Carbohydrates 15 g

Protein 3 g

Listen

6 **Listen to the information about the two soups. Write _L_ for Lundy's
Soup, _C_ for Choice Soup, or _L_ and _C_ for both.**

   _L_ 1.   _____ 3.   _____ 5.   _____ 7.

   _____ 2.   _____ 4.   _____ 6.   _____ 8.

Practice

PAIRS. Compare the nutrition labels for Lundy's Soup and Choice Soup.
Answer the questions. Write _L_ for Lundy's Soup or _C_ for Choice Soup.

1. Which can of soup has more servings?   _L_

2. Which soup has less fat per serving?   _____

3. Which soup has less sodium per serving?   _____

4. Which soup has more protein per serving?   _____

5. Which soup has more carbohydrates per serving?   _____

Make It Yours

GROUPS OF 3. Give your opinion about the two soups. Which soup is healthier? Why?

Example:

A: I think <u>Choice</u> soup is healthier.
B: Why?
A: Because it has <u>less fat</u>.

Choice Soup

NUTRITION FACTS
Serving size ½ cup
Servings per container 3

Calories 100
Calories from Fat 15

Total Fat 1.5 g

Sodium 900 mg

Carbohydrates 10 g

Protein 5 g

Choice
Soup

Lundy's Soup

NUTRITION FACTS
Serving size ½ cup
Servings per container 4

Calories 175
Calories from Fat 35

Total Fat 3.5 g

Sodium 700 mg

Carbohydrates 15 g

Protein 3 g

Lundy's
Soup

BONUS

TEAMS OF 3. Bring in cans, boxes, or packages of at least two different brands of the same food item (soup, cereal, juice, other). Compare the different brands. Ask each other about the information on the labels.

Examples:

What is the weight/size?
How many calories does it have?
How much fat does it have?
Which brand has more calories/fat?
Is it healthy? Why or why not?

Lesson 4 Comparing Values

Learn

> **Note** > > > > > *We write* $7.99/lb. *We say* seven ninety-nine per pound *or* seven ninety-nine a pound. *We write* $3.00/box *or* $3.00/7-oz. box. *We say* three dollars per box, three dollars a box, *or* three dollars for a seven-ounce box.

 7 **Listen and point. Listen and repeat.**

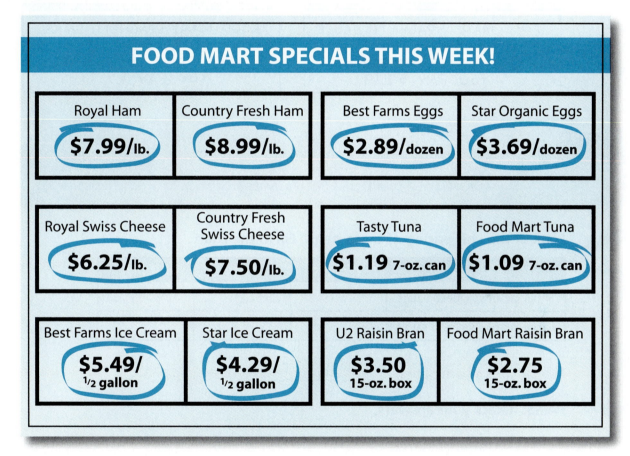

FOOD MART SPECIALS THIS WEEK!

| Royal Ham | Country Fresh Ham | Best Farms Eggs | Star Organic Eggs |
| $7.99/lb. | $8.99/lb. | $2.89/dozen | $3.69/dozen |

| Royal Swiss Cheese | Country Fresh Swiss Cheese | Tasty Tuna | Food Mart Tuna |
| $6.25/lb. | $7.50/lb. | $1.19 7-oz. can | $1.09 7-oz. can |

| Best Farms Ice Cream | Star Ice Cream | U2 Raisin Bran | Food Mart Raisin Bran |
| $5.49/ ½ gallon | $4.29/ ½ gallon | $3.50 15-oz. box | $2.75 15-oz. box |

Practice

A Look at the ads. Look at each pair of items. Which item is less expensive? Check (✓) it.

B *PAIRS.* Check your answers.

> **Example:**
> *A: Royal ham is less expensive than Country Fresh ham.*
> *B: That's correct.*

Learn

FOOD MART SPAGHETTI SAUCE
14 oz.
UNIT PRICE $2.50/lb.
You Pay $2.19

FOOD MART SPAGHETTI SAUCE
25 oz.
UNIT PRICE $1.75/lb.
You Pay $2.73

Note
>>>>> *Supermarkets put a unit pricing label under each item. The unit price helps customers compare prices of different size packages of the same item. Customers can decide, for example, if a large jar of spaghetti sauce (unit price = $1.75/lb.) is a better buy than a small jar (unit price = $2.50/lb.). Sometimes a small jar has a better unit price!*

A **Look at the unit pricing of these items. Fill in the chart.**

	Weight	Price	Unit price
Small jar of spaghetti sauce			
Large jar of spaghetti sauce			

Which jar is a better buy? _____

B *PAIRS.* **Check your answers.**

Practice

A   *PAIRS.* **Read each pair of labels. Circle the letter of the better buy.**

1.

FOOD MART RAISIN BRAN
20 oz.
UNIT PRICE $4.28 PER POUND
You PAY $5.35

a.

FOOD MART RAISIN BRAN
25.5 oz.
UNIT PRICE $3.85 PER POUND
You PAY $6.13

b.

2.

FOOD MART MILK
1/2 GALLON
UNIT PRICE $.99 PER QUART
You PAY $1.98

a.

FOOD MART MILK
1 GALLON
UNIT PRICE $.80 PER QUART
You PAY $3.20

b.

3.

FOOD MART TUNA
7 OZ.
UNIT PRICE $2.72 PER POUND
You PAY $1.19

a.

FOOD MART TUNA
10 OZ.
UNIT PRICE $2.87 PER POUND
You PAY $1.79

b.

B   *PAIRS.* **Check your answers.**

> *Example:*
>
> A: *Which cereal is the better buy?*
> B: *The 25.5-ounce box.*
> A: *That's right.*

Learn

A Read the menu. Answer the questions.

Lou's Café

SPECIAL OF THE DAY $10.95

Soup or salad

Roast Chicken

Choice of vegetable:
peas and carrots,
green beans, or spinach

Choice of potato:
mashed potatoes,
French fries,
or a baked potato

Dessert

Beverage

BURGERS
Classic Beef Burger	$5.50
Mushroom Burger	$6.25
Cheeseburger	$6.50
(American, Cheddar, or Swiss)	
Turkey Burger	$5.50
Deluxe Burger	$7.95

All burgers come with French fries, lettuce and tomato, pickles, and cole slaw.

SANDWICHES
Tuna salad	$5.50
Chicken salad	$6.25
Egg salad	$6.25
Grilled cheese	$4.85
Turkey with lettuce and tomato	$6.95

Choice of bread: white, whole wheat, rye, or a roll. All sandwiches come with cole slaw and pickles.

BEVERAGES
Coffee	$1.50
Tea	$1.50
Soda	$1.75

SOUP
Cup $2.25	Bowl $3.75

Soup of the day (Minestrone)
Chicken Noodle
Vegetable

SIDE ORDERS
French fries	$2.75
Onion rings	$3.25
Garden salad	$3.50
Cole slaw	$1.75

DESSERTS
Fruit pies	$3.25
Rice pudding	$3.75
Chocolate cake	$3.50

1. What is the soup of the day? _____Minestrone._____

2. How much is a bowl of soup? _____

3. What do all sandwiches come with? _____

4. What kind of bread can you have? _____

5. What is the special of the day? _____

6. What are the choices of vegetables? _____

7. Which sandwich is the cheapest? _____

8. Which burger is the most expensive? _____

9. What do they have for dessert? _____

10. How many kinds of burgers do they have? _____

11. How much is a side order of onion rings? _____

12. Do lettuce and tomato cost extra on a turkey sandwich? _____

13. If you order an egg salad sandwich, how much will you pay? _____

B **PAIRS.** Check your answers.

Learn

 8 **Listen. Listen and repeat.**

A: Are you ready to order?

B: Yes, I'd like a <u>hamburger deluxe</u>. Does it come with soup and salad?

A: It comes with <u>French fries, lettuce, tomato, pickles, and cole slaw</u>. Soup or salad is extra.

B: I'll have a cup of soup.

A: Would you like something to drink?

B: Yes, <u>a cup of coffee</u>, please.

A: Anything else?

B. No, thanks.

Practice

PAIRS. **Practice the conversation in Learn. Student A, you are the waitress/ waiter. Student B, order from the menu in Learn. Order a hamburger or a sandwich. Take turns.**

Listen

 9 **Listen. What's the order? Circle *a*, *b*, or *c*.**

1. **a.** a tuna salad sandwich with lettuce

   b. a tuna salad sandwich on rye

   c. a tuna salad sandwich with tomato and lettuce

2. **a.** a hamburger deluxe with a cup of soup and salad

   b. a hamburger deluxe and a cup of coffee

   c. a hamburger deluxe and a cup of soup

3. **a.** a turkey sandwich with fries and coffee

   b. a turkey sandwich with coffee

   c. a turkey sandwich with fries

BONUS *PAIRS.* **Look at the menu. What is your favorite food? Tell your partner.**

Learn

Note
>>>>>
In conversations, people do not always hear or understand what other people say. It is polite to ask Could you repeat that? *or* Did you say . . . ? *to clarify information. You can also repeat the other person's words with rising intonation (a question in your voice).*

 10 **Listen to the conversation. Listen and repeat.**

A: What's the special?
B: It's roast chicken.
A: Did you say **roast** chicken?
B: Yes, **roast** chicken.

A: How much is it?
B: It's $15.99.
A: Could you repeat that?
B: $15.99.

A: What does it come with?
B: It comes with soup or salad.
A: Did you say soup **and** salad?
B: No, soup **or** salad.

A: Does it come with any side orders?
B: It comes with a baked potato and a vegetable.
A: Did you say **baked** potato?
B: Yes, **baked**.

A: You know what, forget the special. I'll have a tuna salad sandwich.

Practice

Early Bird Special

(served from 5:00 P.M. to 6:30 P.M.)

$9.95

SOUP OR SALAD

ENTREES

Broiled salmon with grilled potatoes
or
Roast beef with mashed potatoes
or
Roast chicken with garlic mashed potatoes

Broccoli

DESSERT
chocolate cake or apple pie

COFFEE, TEA, OR SODA

A  CD2 TRACK 11 **Listen to the conversation. Listen and repeat.**

A: What does the salmon come with?
B: It comes with <u>grilled potatoes</u> and broccoli.
A: With **grilled** potatoes?
B: Yes, grilled potatoes and broccoli.

B *PAIRS.* **Practice the conversation. Use other entrees from the menu. Use rising intonation to ask for clarification.**

Make It Yours

PAIRS. **Write a new conversation between a waiter/waitress and a customer. Use *Could you repeat that?* or *Did you say . . . ?* to ask for clarification.**

BONUS *GROUPS OF 3.* **What are some other ways to ask for clarification? Make a list and report back to the class.**

Unit 5 Test

Before you take the test

ⒶⒷⒸⒹ Use the answer sheet for Unit 5 on page 211.

1. Print your name.
2. Print your teacher's name.
3. Write your student identification number, and bubble in the information below the boxes.
4. Write the test date and bubble in the information.
5. Write your class number and bubble in the information.

Listening I [Tracks 12–15]

Look at the pictures and listen. What is the correct answer: A, B, or C?

1.

| A | B | C |

2.

GOOD RICE — Ingredients: white rice — Net Wt. 13 oz. — **A**

A-OK RICE — Ingredients: white rice — Net Wt. 16 oz. — **B**

Tasty Rice — Ingredients: white rice — Net Wt. 18 oz. — **C**

3.

YUMMY PEACH ICE CREAM 1 QUART — UNIT PRICE $ .18/oz. — **A**

YUMMY CHOCOLATE ICE CREAM 1/2 GALLON — UNIT PRICE $ .17/oz. — **B**

YUMMY STRAWBERRY ICE CREAM 1 GALLON — UNIT PRICE $ .12/oz. — **C**

You will hear a conversation.
Then you will hear a question about the conversation.
What is the correct answer: A, B, or C?

4. A. 8 ounces

   B. $3.99

   C. 1 pound

5. A. 1 gallon

   B. 3 quarts

   C. ½ gallon

6. A. Best Bread.

   B. Star Bread.

   C. The prices are the same.

7. A. a hamburger with onions

   B. a hamburger with onions and a soda

   C. a hamburger and French fries

8. A. Grilled chicken with salad.

   B. Soup and salad.

   C. The total is $5.50.

Reading

Read. What is the correct answer? A, B, C, or D?

Bill's

Best Beans

Nutrition facts:
Serving size: ½ c.
Servings per container: 8
Calories per serving: 180
Total fat per serving: 1 g.
Sodium per serving: 800 mg.
Protein per serving: 6 g.

32 oz.

---

9. How many servings are there in this can of beans?

    A. ½

    B. 180

    C. 6

    D. 8

10. How much protein per serving do these beans have?

    A. 180 grams

    B. 6 grams

    C. 8 grams

    D. 1 gram

11. How many pounds of beans are in this can?

    A. 2½

    B. 2

    C. ½

    D. 32

12. Which drink is a better buy?

    A. Yummy Chocolate Milk.

    B. Fudgy Chocolate Milk.

    C. The unit price is the same.

    D. Yummy Chocolate Milk weighs more.

13. Which bottle has more chocolate milk?

    A. The unit price is $.14/oz.

    B. Fudgy Chocolate Milk.

    C. Yummy Chocolate Milk.

    D. The unit price is $.12/oz.

Americana Lunch Menu

Spaghetti with marinara sauce $6.49

Hamburger with onions $7.29

Deli salad with ham and cheese $5.95

Fish sandwich with tartar sauce $6.99

All meals are served with your choice of cole slaw, French fries, or side salad.

14. Which lunch is the most expensive?

A. the hamburger

B. the deli salad

C. the fish sandwich

D. the spaghetti

15. What comes with each meal?

A. French fries

B. French fries, cole slaw, or a side salad

C. cole slaw and French fries

D. a side salad

Unit 6 Money and Shopping

Lesson 1   **Using an ATM**
- Use an ATM

Lesson 2   **Reading Receipts**
- Read a receipt and compute discounts

Lesson 3   **Writing Checks**
- Read and fill out a check

Lesson 4   **Shopping**
- Ask about availability of items in a store

Lesson 5   **Returning and Exchanging Purchases**
- Give reasons for returning or exchanging an item

Learn

A **Read the paragraph. Then match the words or phrases with their explanations.**

Laura likes to use the ATM (automated teller machine) at her bank because it is available 24/7—twenty-four hours a day, seven days a week. She can deposit money or make a withdrawal. She can also transfer money from one of her accounts to another. For example, she can move money from her savings account to her checking account. She can also check her account balance and get a printed statement. To use the machine, she puts in her card, enters her PIN (Personal Identification Number), and then follows directions on the screen by pressing buttons for different options. An ATM is usually free, but sometimes Laura pays a small fee to use an ATM at a different bank where she doesn't have her accounts.

_h_ 1. insert your card

____ 2. PIN

____ 3. deposit money

____ 4. make a withdrawal

____ 5. transfer funds

____ 6. account balance

____ 7. statement

____ 8. fee

a. move money from one account to another

b. how much money you have in your account

c. take out money from your account

d. a list of the transactions in your account

e. money you pay for a service

f. your secret password or number

g. put money into your account

h. put your ATM card into the machine

B *PAIRS.* **Check your answers.**

> **Example**
>
> A: Insert your card *means put your ATM card into the machine.*
> B: *That's right.*

C **Read the paragraph again. Answer the questions.**

1. Why does Laura like to use an ATM for her banking? _____

2. What transactions can she do at an ATM? _____

3. What does she do first to use an ATM? _____

4. What does she enter after she puts in her card? _____

5. Which ATMs sometimes charge a fee? _____

D  22 Listen to the directions to withdraw money. Point to the choices on the screens.

Insert your card

Enter your Personal Identification Number, using the keypad.

How can we help you?
Select your choice.
- Make a Deposit
- Make a Withdrawal
- Transfer Funds
- Get Balance Info
- Get a Statement
- Start Over

Select an account.

- Savings
- Checking

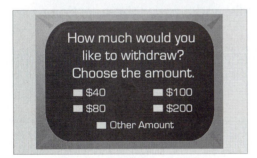

How much would you like to withdraw?
Choose the amount.
- $40
- $80
- $100
- $200
- Other Amount

Please take your card, cash, and receipt.

Practice

A Put the directions to withdraw money in the correct order. Number the steps in order from 1 to 6.

_____ Choose *Make a Withdrawal*.

_____ Take out your card, the money, and the receipt.

__1__ Insert your card.

_____ Select *Checking*.

_____ Enter your PIN, using the keypad.

_____ Choose the amount to withdraw: *$40*.

B *PAIRS.* Check your answers.

Learn

A   **Look at the ads. Answer the questions.**

> **Buy one, get one**
> **free with coupon!**
> Forest Glen Shampoo
> $2.89 11-oz. bottle.
> **SECOND BOTTLE FREE!**

> **Buy one, get one**
> **50% off with coupon!**
> Honey Crackers
> $4.00/pkg.
> **SECOND PACKAGE**
> **50% OFF!**

> **SALE!**
> Bay Paper Towels
> Pkg. of 8 rolls reg. $6.99.
> **THIS WEEK ONLY**
> **$5.69!**

1. You buy two bottles of shampoo. How much will you pay? $2.89

2. You buy two packages of Honey Crackers. How much will you pay? $ _____

3. What is the regular price for a package of eight rolls of Bay Paper Towels? $ _____

B   **Read the receipt. Check the prices carefully and answer the questions.**

Note >>>>> T *means that an item is taxable. Most states have a sales tax, but some do not.*

1. How many taxable items are there? ___13___

2. What is the total before tax? _____

3. How much is the tax? _____

4. What is the total bill? _____

5. How much change do you get if you give the cashier $40? _____

```
        Forest Drugstore

1 Forest Glen Shampoo 11 oz.        2.89 T
1 Forest Glen Shampoo 11 oz.        2.89 T
                                   -2.89
            CPN (Buy 1 get 1 free.)

1 KS Shaving Cream 10 oz.           1.49 T
1 Daisy 1% Milk 64 oz.              3.29
1 Bay Paper Towels 8 Rolls          5.69 T
                                    SALE

1 Honey Crackers                    4.00
1 Honey Crackers                    4.00
                                   -2.00
        CPN (Buy 1 get 2nd 50% off)

3 CJ Toothpaste @ 2/4.00            6.00 T

2 NRG Bars 5/4.00                   1.60
2 lb. BK Candy @ 3.50/lb.           7.00 T

           13 ITEMS
              SUBTOTAL    33.96
              TAX 5%       1.15
              TOTAL       35.11
              CASH        40.00
              CHANGE       4.89
```

Practice

PAIRS. **Look at the sale price of each item. Calculate the total cost of the item(s). Fill in the amounts.**

1.
> SK Toothpaste $2.35
> Buy 1 get 1 free.

2 SK Toothpaste $ <u>2.35</u>

2.
> SK Shampoo 16 oz. $4.00
> Buy 1 get 50% off 2nd.

2 SK Shampoo $ _____

3.
> PG Orange Juice 64 oz. 2/$5.00

1 PG Orange Juice $ _____

4.
> RG Deodorant 8 oz. $1.50

3 RG Deodorant $ _____

5.
> BL Toothbrushes 4/$4.00

5 BL Toothbrushes $ _____

6.
> SK Cleaner $5.99
> SK Cleaner coupon $1.00 off

SK Cleaner $ _____

Make It Yours

PAIRS **Look at the drugstore ad. Then look at the receipt. Two prices on the receipt are wrong. Find them and circle them.**

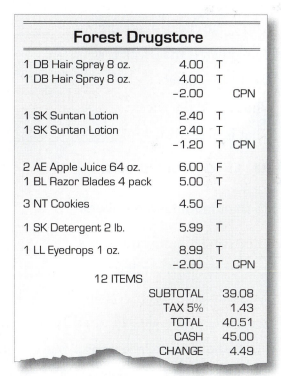

Forest Drugstore

1 DB Hair Spray 8 oz.	4.00	T
1 DB Hair Spray 8 oz.	4.00	T
	-2.00	CPN
1 SK Suntan Lotion	2.40	T
1 SK Suntan Lotion	2.40	T
	-1.20	T CPN
2 AE Apple Juice 64 oz.	6.00	F
1 BL Razor Blades 4 pack	5.00	T
3 NT Cookies	4.50	F
1 SK Detergent 2 lb.	5.99	T
1 LL Eyedrops 1 oz.	8.99	T
	-2.00	T CPN
12 ITEMS		
SUBTOTAL	39.08	
TAX 5%	1.43	
TOTAL	40.51	
CASH	45.00	
CHANGE	4.49	

BONUS *TEAMS OF 3.* **Think about shopping in supermarkets and drugstores. Talk about the following questions:**

Do you always check your receipts? Do you ever find mistakes on your receipts? When? What do you do if you find a mistake?

Learn

```
David Camacho                                              101
123 Appleton St.
Miami, FL 33121                             November 1, 2007

PAY TO THE
ORDER OF    Union Gas                              | $  246.23

Two Hundred Forty-six and 23/100 _____  DOLLARS

ELM BANK
49-22 Victor Street
Miami, FL 33125

FOR ____ Acc. #624135 _____      David Camacho _____

4:3788825424: 3|||971335|||01
```

A **Look at the check and answer the questions.**

1. Who is the check made out to? _____ Union Gas _____

2. How much is the check for? _____

3. What is the date? _____

4. Who signed the check? _____

5. What is Acc. #624135? _____

B *PAIRS.* **Check your answers.**

C **Write the amounts in numbers.**

1. Fifteen and $^{00}/_{100}$ dollars _____ $15.00 _____

2. Fifty-one and $^{15}/_{100}$ dollars _____

3. One Hundred Ninety-five and $^{08}/_{100}$ dollars _____

4. Two Thousand Eight Hundred Twenty-six and $^{34}/_{100}$ dollars _____

5. Three Thousand Nineteen and $^{65}/_{100}$ dollars _____

6. Four Thousand Forty-two and $^{50}/_{100}$ dollars _____

D *PAIRS.* **Check your answers.**

Practice

A   Write these amounts in words and numbers.

1. $16.00   _____ *Sixteen and* $^{00}/_{100}$ _____   DOLLARS

2. $82.25   _____   DOLLARS

3. $160.50   _____   DOLLARS

4. $700.00   _____   DOLLARS

5. $689.93   _____   DOLLARS

6. $3,257.66   _____   DOLLARS

B   *PAIRS.* **Check your answers.**

C   **Fill out the check with the following information. Use today's date and sign your name.**

- Marin Management
- $982.15
- rent

D   *PAIRS.* **Check your answers.**

Make It Yours

Fill out these two checks for expenses that you have next month. (It's OK to use made-up information.)

		105

_____ 20 _____

PAY TO THE
ORDER OF _____ $ [ ]

_____ DOLLARS

ELM BANK
49-22 Victor Street
Miami, FL 33125

FOR _____ _____

4:3788825424: 3⏐⏐⏐971335⏐⏐⏐05

		106

_____ 20 _____

PAY TO THE
ORDER OF _____ $ [ ]

_____ DOLLARS

ELM BANK
49-22 Victor Street
Miami, FL 33125

FOR _____ _____

4:3788825424: 3⏐⏐⏐971335⏐⏐⏐06

BONUS *PAIRS.* **How do you pay your bills? By money order? By check? In cash? Discuss.**

Learn

 23 **Listen to the conversation. Listen and repeat.**

A: Do you have these shoes in size 6?
B: Let me check in the back.
A: Do you have them in purple?
B: Sorry, only black or blue.
A: And, do you carry Venus sandals?
B: Yes, but they're not in stock.

Practice

PAIRS. **Practice the conversation in Learn. Then make new conversations with these items.**

1. **I'll have to check in the back.**

2. **Yes, we have them in stock. Let me get them.**

3. **Yes, we have them in black or white.**

4. **Sorry, we're out of that size.**

5. **Sorry, they're not in stock.**

6. **Sorry, we don't carry them.**

Listen

 24 **Listen. What do you hear? Circle *a*, *b*, or *c*.**

1. **a.** She wants sandals.　　**b.** She wants boots.　　**c.** She wants shoes.

2. **a.** He has the shoes in white.　　**b.** He doesn't have the shoes in white.　　**c.** He is looking in the back.

3. **a.** size 8　　**b.** size 6　　**c.** size 9

4. **a.** The boots are in stock in the back.　　**b.** The boots aren't in stock.　　**c.** The boots are on the shelf on the left.

Returning and Exchanging Purchases

Learn

 25 **Listen to the conversation. Listen and repeat.**

A: I'd like to return this <u>toaster</u>. <u>It doesn't work.</u>
B: Do you want to exchange it, or get a refund?
A: I'd like a refund.
B: Do you have the receipt?
A: Yes. Here it is.

Practice

A Fill in the blanks. Use the words and sentences in the boxes.

microwave
blender
iron
coffeemaker

It leaks.
There is a part missing.
It doesn't fit in my kitchen.
It doesn't turn off.

1. _____

2. _____

3. _____

4. _____

B **PAIRS.** Practice the conversation in Learn. Use the items and the problems in the pictures.

C   Read the paragraph. Then answer the questions. Circle *a*, *b*, or *c*.

Shoppers Town Department Store
Return and Exchange Policy

Any merchandise from Shoppers Town may be returned
or exchanged at a store within 90 days of purchase.
Returns and exchanges must be new, unused, and contain
all packaging. Some items cannot be returned if they are
opened, such as music, movies, video games, and software.
A receipt is required for returns and exchanges.
If customers do not have receipts, they can show a
canceled check or the credit card bill for the purchase.

---

1. What is the longest you can wait to return or exchange an item?

    a. ninety days   **b.** thirty days   **c.** sixty days

2. What can't you return?

    a. CDs that are on sale   **b.** CDs that you didn't open   **c.** CDs that you listened to, but you don't like

3. If you don't have a receipt, what can you show the sales clerk?

    a. a canceled check   **b.** a driver's license   **c.** a passport

4. Which item can be returned or exchanged?

    a. a DVD you bought last week and never opened   **b.** a coat you bought six months ago   **c.** a coffeemaker without its orginal box

---

BONUS   **GROUPS OF 3. Discuss your experiences with returning items.**

What items did you return?

Did you exchange the items or get a refund?

Were there any problems when you returned the item?

Unit 6 Test

Listening I [Tracks 26–30]

Listen to the sentence.
Which of the following means the same as the sentence you heard: A, B, or C?

1. A. The ATM is available 24 days per month.

   B. The ATM is available 4 days per week.

   C. The ATM is available 7 days per week and 24 hours per day.

2. A. The store doesn't have crackers.

   B. The crackers are free.

   C. The crackers are half price.

3. A. Paper towels are cheaper this week.

   B. Paper towels are half price.

   C. Buy one, get one free.

4. A. She paid $78.

   B. She paid cash.

   C. She needs to check the bill.

Listening II [Tracks 31–33]

Listen. Everything is on the audio CD.

Reading

Read. What is the correct answer: A, B, C, or D?

Nick is nineteen years old and works at a restaurant. When he gets his paycheck, he goes to the ATM at his bank and deposits it into his bank account. He can check his bank balance to see how much money he has.

Nick often goes to the ATM at the bank and withdraws money so he can buy gas for his car and go out with his friends after work. When he can't get to the bank, Nick goes to an ATM at the gas station or the supermarket. He has to pay a fee when he doesn't use the bank's ATM, but he likes the convenience of getting money any time.

---

7. What can Nick do at the ATM?

   A. deposit and withdraw money

   B. deposit money

   C. deposit and withdraw money and check his balance

   D. withdraw money and check his balance

8. Where does Nick get money when he can't go to the bank?

   A. from his parents

   B. at ATMs in stores or gas stations

   C. at his job

   D. from his friends

```
More 4 Less

606 N. Ball Road
Greenhill, CA 92333
Tel 210-555-9889


848    Shiny Shampoo          5.38
       discount              −3.40

232    Shiny Conditioner      5.38
       discount              −3.40


              Subtotal        3.96
              CA tax           .31
              Total           4.27


You saved $6.80 on sale items!
Thank you. Please come again
```

9. How much money did the customer save on the Shiny Conditioner?

    A. $5.38

    B. $3.40

    C. $3.96

    D. $4.27

10. How much total money did the customer save?

    A. $3.40

    B. $3.96

    C. $.31

    D. $6.80

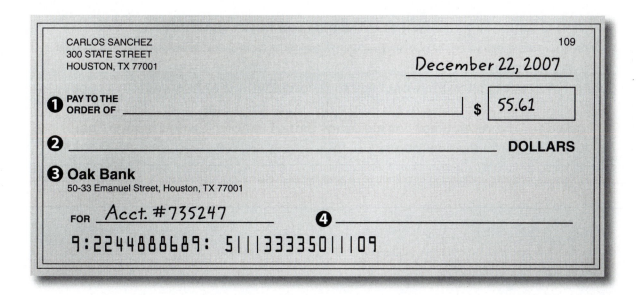

CARLOS SANCHEZ
300 STATE STREET
HOUSTON, TX 77001

109

December 22, 2007

① PAY TO THE ORDER OF _____ $ | 55.61

② _____ **DOLLARS**

③ Oak Bank
50-33 Emanuel Street, Houston, TX 77001

FOR *Acct. #735247* **④** _____

⑨:2244888689: 5III333350II109

11. What should Carlos write on line 2?

    A. Fifty-five and 61/100

    B. $55.61

    C. My Favorite Gift Shop

    D. One hundred dollars

12. What should Carlos write on line 4?

    A. Fifty-five and 61/100

    B. the date

    C. the name of the store

    D. his signature

Joe bought a pair of shoes at the mall last week. The shoes were a nice color and a good price. When he got home, he tried the shoes on again. They were too tight.

Two weeks later, Joe went back to the mall with the shoes and his receipt. He asked the sales clerk to exchange the shoes for a bigger size. The clerk asked for the receipt and got Joe a new pair of shoes. Now Joe is happy and comfortable in his new shoes.

13. Why did Joe exchange his shoes?

    A. The shoes were too big.

    B. The shoes were too small.

    C. The shoes were too expensive.

    D. He wanted a different color.

14. What did Joe give the sales clerk?

    A. his paycheck

    B. his phone number

    C. his receipt

    D. his driver's license

Unit 7

Understanding Measurements

Lesson 1 **Temperatures in Fahrenheit and Celsius**
- **Understand temperatures in Fahrenheit and Celsius**

Lesson 2 **Measuring Dimensions**
- **Use the American system of measuring dimensions**

Lesson 3 **Measuring Distance**
- **Use the American system of measuring distance**

Learn

 34 Listen and point. Listen and repeat.

> **Note**
> >>>>> In the United States, temperature is measured in degrees Fahrenheit. Normal body temperature is 98.6°F, water freezes at 32°F, and water boils at 212°F.

WEATHER	FAHRENHEIT	CELSIUS
It's very hot.	100°F	38°C
It's hot.	90°F	32°C
It's warm.	70°F	21°C
It's cool.	50°F	10°C
It's cold.	32°F	0°C
It's very cold.	0°F	−18°C

Practice

A **35** Listen to the conversation. Listen and repeat.

A: How is it outside today?
B: It's about <u>70 degrees</u>.
A: Oh, it's <u>warm</u>.

B *PAIRS.* Practice the conversation. Use other temperatures and weather words from Learn.

Listen

36 Listen to the sentences. Circle the letter of the temperature that matches.

1.   **a.** It's 38°.   **b.** It's 68°.
2.   **a.** It's 98°.   **b.** It's 70°.
3.   **a.** It's 89°.   **b.** It's 40°.
4.   **a.** It's 16°.   **b.** It's 71°.
5.   **a.** It's 62°.   **b.** It's 22°.

Make It Yours

GROUPS OF 3. **Look at the temperatures. Make a list of the clothes people wear.**

19°F	45°F	88°F

BONUS   *GROUPS OF 3.* **What temperature do you like in your house? Discuss and then report to the class.**

Learn

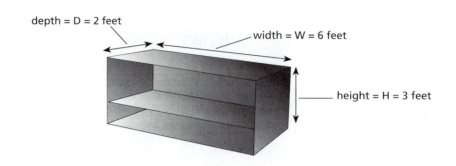

depth = D = 2 feet

width = W = 6 feet

height = H = 3 feet

Note
>>>>> *We measure height, width, and depth in feet and inches. We measure a few things, like fabric, in yards and feet.*

A  **37** **Listen to the measurements. Listen and repeat.**

		1 inch	(2.54 centimeters)
	1 foot	12 inches	(0.3 meters)
1 yard	3 feet	36 inches	(about 1 meter)

B **Match the measurements.**

  _b_ 1. 24 inches   a. 6 feet

  ____ 2. 36 inches   b. 2 feet

  ____ 3. 4 yards   c. 3 feet

  ____ 4. 2 yards   d. 12 feet

  ____ 5. 12 inches   e. 1 foot

Note
>>>>> *The symbol for feet is ft. or '. The symbol for inches is in. or ".*

C **38** **Look at the picture of a bookcase. Listen to the conversation. Listen and repeat.**

A: How wide is the bookcase?
B: It's thirty-eight inches wide.
A: How deep is it?
B: It's thirteen inches deep.
A: How tall is it?
B: It's sixty-eight inches tall.

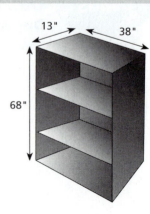

13"   38"

68"

Practice

A   *PAIRS.* **Cover your partner's information. Student A, ask Student B the dimensions of the dresser. Ask questions with *How*. Write the answers on the picture. Student B, ask Student A the dimensions of the refrigerator. Ask questions with *How*. Write the answers on the picture.**

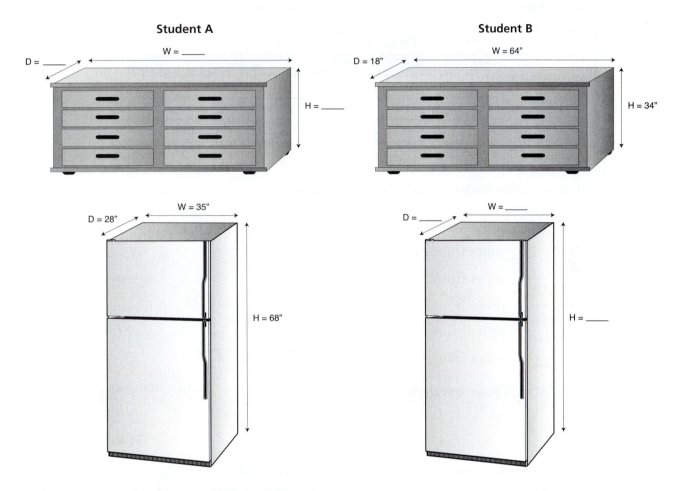

Student A

W = _____
D = _____
H = _____

W = 35"
D = 28"
H = 68"

Student B

W = 64"
D = 18"
H = 34"

W = _____
D = _____
H = _____

B   *PAIRS.* **Check your answers.**

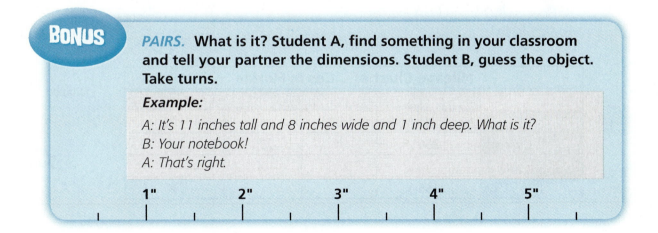

BONUS   *PAIRS.* **What is it? Student A, find something in your classroom and tell your partner the dimensions. Student B, guess the object. Take turns.**

Example:

A: It's 11 inches tall and 8 inches wide and 1 inch deep. What is it?
B: Your notebook!
A: That's right.

1"   2"   3"   4"   5"

Learn

A   What is the distance between Houston and San Antonio? Look at the chart. The answer is *200 miles.* How do you know?

Mileage Chart of Cities in Texas

	Austin	Dallas	Houston	San Antonio
Austin	X	190	160	80
Dallas	190	X	250	270
Houston	160	250	X	200
San Antonio	80	270	200	X

B   Fill in the information, using the mileage chart.

1. It's __200__ miles from Houston to San Antonio.

2. It's _____ miles from Austin to Houston.

3. It's _____ miles from Austin to San Antonio.

4. It's _____ miles from Dallas to Houston.

5. It's _____ miles from Dallas to San Antonio.

6. It's _____ miles from Austin to Dallas.

C   *PAIRS.* Check your answers.

• Dallas

• Austin

• Houston

San Antonio

Practice

PAIRS. Student A, look at the mileage chart below. Student B, look at the mileage chart on page 111. Ask each other questions to complete both charts.

Example:

A: How far is Orlando from Jacksonville?
B: It's 140 miles.

Tallahassee

Jacksonville

Orlando

Miami

Mileage Chart of Cities in Florida

	Jacksonville	Miami	Orlando	Tallahassee
Jacksonville	X	350	140	165
Miami	350	X	235	
Orlando		235	X	
Tallahassee	165			X

Mileage Chart of Cities in Florida				
	Jacksonville	**Miami**	**Orlando**	**Tallahassee**
Jacksonville	X		140	
Miami		X		480
Orlando	140		X	260
Tallahassee		480	260	X

Make It Yours

PAIRS. **Ask each other distances from one place to another.**

> *Example:*
>
> A: *How far is your house from the school?*
> B: *It's about 10 miles. How far is your hometown from here?*
> A: *It's about 3,000 miles.*

Listen

 39 **Listen. What do you hear? Circle *a* or *b*.**

1. **a.** 118 **b.** 180

2. **a.** 40 **b.** 14

3. **a.** 155 **b.** 165

4. **a.** 66 **b.** 76

5. **a.** 31 **b.** 301

BONUS
About how many kilometers per hour is 55 miles per hour?

a. about 68km/h b. about 78km/h c. about 88km/h

Answer: c

Unit 7 Test

 Listening I [Tracks 40–43]

Listen to the sentence.
Which of the following means the same as the sentence
you heard: A, B, or C?

1. A. It's 100°F.

   B. It's 0°C.

   C. It's 50°F.

2. A. It's 3°C.

   B. It's 36 inches wide.

   C. It's 3 miles long.

3. A. What's the weather today?

   B. Do you want to go outside?

   C. Take your coat.

 Listening II [Tracks 44–46]

Listen. Everything is on the audio CD.

Reading

Read. What is the correct answer: A, B, C, or D?

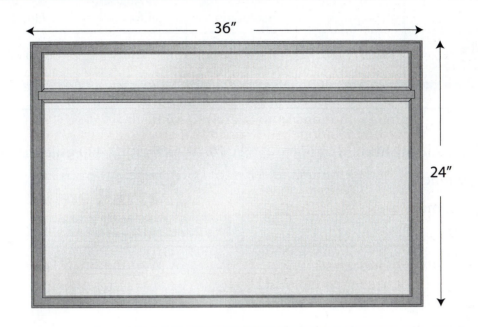

6. How wide is the window?

    A. 36 feet

    B. 2 feet

    C. 24 inches

    D. 36 inches

7. What is the height of the window?

    A. 36 inches

    B. 24 inches

    C. 36 feet

    D. 24 feet

8. Which measurement is the same as 36 inches?

    A. 1 yard

    B. 2 yards

    C. 3 yards

    D. 1 foot

U.S. Cities Mileage Chart

	Washington, D.C.	Denver, Colorado	Los Angeles, California	Miami, Florida
Albany, New York	400 miles	1,830 miles	2,850 miles	1,400 miles

9. How far is Albany from Miami?

    A. 400 miles

    B. 2,850 miles

    C. 1,830 miles

    D. 1,400 miles

10. Which city is 400 miles from Albany?

    A. Miami

    B. Los Angeles

    C. Denver

    D. Washington, D.C.

Unit 8 Housing

Lesson 1 **Finding an Apartment for Rent**
- **Read signs and ads for apartments**

Lesson 2 **Renting an Apartment**
- **Describe and ask about an apartment for rent**

Lesson 3 **Housing Problems**
- **Describe common problems in an apartment**

Learn

 A   **Teresa needs an apartment. Read the story.**

> Teresa is looking for an apartment in Linden. She wants an apartment that is near transportation because she doesn't have a car. She likes one apartment in the center of town. It is a large one-bedroom apartment with a living room, a kitchen, and a dining room. It has air-conditioning, a dishwasher, and a washer and dryer in the basement. The rent is $1,200 a month including heat and hot water. If she takes the apartment, she has to give 1½ months' security deposit. The apartment is available now, but Teresa is going to look a little more.

B   **Read the story again. Read the sentences. Circle *T* for *True* or *F* for *False*.**

1. Teresa needs to live near transportation.   (T)   F

2. She likes an apartment far from the center of town.   T   F

3. The apartment has four rooms.   T   F

4. The apartment has air-conditioning.   T   F

5. There is a washer and dryer in the apartment.   T   F

6. She has to pay for electricity.   T   F

7. The security deposit is $1,200.   T   F

8. The apartment isn't available yet.   T   F

Read the classified ad for the apartment. Match the abbreviations to their meanings.

FOR RENT

Lg. 2 BR, DR, 1½ BA, a/c, dw,
w/d in bsmt., $900 incl. h/hw,
nr. trans., avail. immed.,
1½ mo. sec.,
Call eves. 419-555-1515

_e_ 1. a/c   a. $900, heat and hot water are included

____ 2. lg. 2 BR   b. available immediately

____ 3. avail. immed.   c. dishwasher

____ 4. nr. trans.   d. large two-bedroom apartment

____ 5. dw   e. air-conditioning

____ 6. $900 incl. h/hw   f. near transportation

____ 7. 1½ mo. sec.   g. dining room

____ 8. w/d in bsmt.   h. washer and dryer in basement

____ 9. eves.   i. 1½ months' security deposit required

____ 10. DR   j. bathroom

____ 11. BA   k. evenings

Listen

47 **Listen to the conversations. What do you hear? Circle *a, b,* or *c.***

1. **a.** two bedrooms   **b.** two bathrooms   **c.** air-conditioning

2. **a.** a dishwasher   **b.** a washer and dryer   **c.** air-conditioning

3. **a.** heat and hot water **b.** electricity   **c.** air-conditioning

4. **a.** parking   **b.** a park   **c.** near train station

Practice

A Look at the apartment ads. Read the situation for each person. Match the people with the best apartment for them.

Lg. 1 BR apt.,
1 mo. sec.,
avail. end of month,
couple pref.,
$850 month + utilities,
a/c, dw, w/d, no pets.
Call super after 6 P.M.

a.

2 BR, LR, DR,
1½ baths,
a/c, dw, w/d,
$1,300 incl. h/hw,
avail. immed.

1 BR apt., 1 mo.

b.

Call super.

Studio,
a/c, dw,
$700 incl.
h/hw, nr. trans.

c.

_____ 1. Clara and Bob are married and have two children, a son who is ten years old and a daughter who is five years old. They can pay about $1,400 a month for rent and utilities. They need to move soon.

_____ 2. Lynn is twenty-five years old and is single. She works downtown. She doesn't have a car. She has a dog. She can pay about $800 a month for rent and utilities. She needs to move next month.

_____ 3. Victor and Maria just got married. They are looking for an apartment. They can pay about $1,100 a month for rent and utilities.

B *PAIRS.* **Explain why you matched each classified ad with the person**

> **Example:**
>
> A: The best apartment for Clara and Bob is _____ because it _____.
> B: I agree. (or) I disagree.

Make It Yours

A Write an ad for an apartment or house you want.

B *PAIRS.* Tell your partner about the apartment.

Learn

 Note >>>>> *People find apartments from friends, newspaper classified ads, ads on the Internet, and real estate agencies. Real estate agencies charge a fee if they find an apartment for you. It's a good idea to look at more than one apartment before renting. Compare the rents, the neighborhoods, and the schools.*

A **48** **Listen to the conversation. Listen and repeat.**

A: Hello?
B: Hello, I'm calling about the apartment for rent.
A: Yes?
B: It's a <u>two-bedroom</u> apartment?
A: That's right. And it has a <u>kitchen, living room, and one and a half bathrooms</u>.
B: OK. I'm interested in seeing the apartment.
A: How's <u>tomorrow at 7 P.M.</u>?
B: That's fine. What's the address?
A: <u>1515 Banyon Street.</u>
B: <u>1515 Banyon</u>. Great. See you tomorrow at <u>7</u>.

B *PAIRS.* **Practice the conversation.**

Make It Yours

PAIRS. **Bring in newspaper apartment ads and practice calling for information about an apartment for rent. Make an appointment to see the apartment.**

 BONUS | *GROUPS OF 3.* **Talk about your apartment/house and neighborhood.**

Do you live in an apartment or a house?

How did you find your apartment or house?

Why did you choose your apartment or house?

How are the schools in your area?

What is your dream apartment or house?

Learn

A CD2 TRACK **49** Look at the problems. Listen and point. Listen and repeat.

_____ A pipe in my kitchen is leaking.

_____ My toilet is overflowing.

_____ My toilet isn't flushing.

_____ The faucet in my bathtub is dripping.

_____ My refrigerator isn't working.

_____ The plaster is falling from my bedroom ceiling.

_____ My kitchen sink is stopped up.

_____ My bedroom door is stuck.

_____ My front door lock is broken.

B CD2 TRACK **50** Listen and number the pictures in the order that you hear them.

Practice

Note
> > > > >

When there is a problem in your apartment, call the building manager. If there is no answer, write a note. If there is still no answer, send a registered letter. Keep a record of the date. When the problem is serious (for example, no heat in the winter), look in the Blue Pages of your phone book and call a city agency.

A **51** Listen to the conversation. Listen and repeat.

A: Hello. This is <u>Mr. Kim</u> in apartment 3E.
B: Yes, Mr. Kim. How can I help you?
A: <u>A pipe in my kitchen is leaking.</u>
B: I'll try to come by tomorrow.
A: How about this afternoon?
B: Sorry, I can't. How's tomorrow at 10 A.M.?
A: I'll see you then.

B *PAIRS.* **Practice the conversation, using other problems from Learn. Use your names. Take turns.**

Listen

 52 Listen to the conversations. What do you hear? Circle *a*, *b*, or *c*.

1. What is the problem?
   a. The faucet is leaking.   **b.** The toilet is leaking.   **c.** The faucet is dripping.

2. What is the problem?
   a. The toilet is stopped up.   **b.** The toilet is overflowing.   **c.** The toilet isn't flushing.

3. What is the problem?
   a. The window is broken.   **b.** The window is stuck.   **c.** The lock is stuck.

Make It Yours

What are some other problems in apartments? Make your own sentences.

_____ is broken.
_____ isn't working.
_____ is leaking.
_____ is stopped up.

 BONUS *GROUPS OF 3.* **What problems have you had with apartments in the past? Discuss.**

Unit 8 Test

Listening I [Tracks 53–56]

Listen to the first part of the conversation.
What should the person say next: A, B, or C?

1. A. They have to pay rent in cash.

B. How about tomorrow at 10 A.M.?

C. It's a small house.

2. A. I'll be over at 1 P.M.

B. The toilet is leaking.

C. Let's go to dinner.

3. A. Then the rent is too high.

B. See you at 7 P.M. tomorrow.

C. They have to give a deposit.

Listening II [Tracks 57–60]

Listen. Everything is on the audio CD.

Reading

Read. What is the correct answer? A, B, C, or D?

Apartments for Rent

❶ Laguna Beach, 2 BR, 2 BA, $1,600, ocean view, small pets OK

❷ Newport Beach, 3 BR, 2 BA, $2,100, no pets, avail. immed.

❸ Fox Road, 2 BR, 1 BA, DR, 2-car gar., $1,350, pets OK

All apartments have a dishwasher.
Rent includes utilities.
1 1/2 months security deposit required.
Call 901-555-2222 today!

---

7. Which apartments have two bedrooms?

    A. apartments 1 and 2

    B. apartments 2 and 3

    C. apartments 1 and 3

    D. all of them

8. Which apartment is available immediately?

    A. all of them

    B. none of them

    C. apartment 2

    D. apartment 3

9. What is included with each apartment?

    A. two bathrooms

    B. pets

    C. a garage

    D. a dishwasher

Goldenview Apartment Repair Request
Telephone Message

Date: November 12, 2007

While you were out: Monica Torres

   in Apt. # 6B **called.**

Phone: 555-9987

Problem: Yesterday the pipe under my kitchen sink began to leak. Also, the toilet isn't flushing. Please come soon!

10. What is one of the problems in Monica's apartment?

   A. The rent is late.

   B. There's a washer and dryer.

   C. Her refrigerator is broken.

   D. A pipe is leaking.

11. What other problem does Monica have in her apartment?

   A. The toilet is leaking.

   B. The toilet isn't flushing.

   C. The toilet is running.

   D. The toilet is in the kitchen.

Unit 9 — Health

Lesson 1   **Parts of the Body**
- Identify parts of the body
- Identify parts of the face

Lesson 2   **Injuries**
- Learn words to talk about injuries

Lesson 3   **Feeling Sick**
- Identify common symptoms

Lesson 4   **Making an Appointment**
- Make an appointment with the doctor

Lesson 5   **Medical History Forms**
- Fill out a medical history form
- Identify common diseases and conditions

Lesson 6   **Medicine**
- Identify common prescription and nonprescription medicines

Lesson 7   **Medicine Labels**
- Read medicine labels, including dosages

Learn

A Look at the pictures. Write the words on the lines. For an extra challenge, cover the words in the box when you write.

ankle	chest	hand	neck	throat
back	elbow	~~head~~	shoulder	thumb
breast	finger	hip	stomach	toe
buttocks	foot	knee	thigh	wrist

1. *head*
2. _____
3. _____
4. _____
5. _____
6. _____
7. _____
8. _____
9. _____
10. _____
11. _____

12. _____
13. _____
14. _____
15. _____
16. _____
17. _____
18. _____
19. _____
20. _____

B Listen and check your answers. Listen and repeat.

Learn

A   Look at the picture. Write the words on the lines. For an extra
challenge, cover the words in the box when you write.

cheek	eye	~~forehead~~
chin	eyebrow	lips
ear	eyelashes	nose

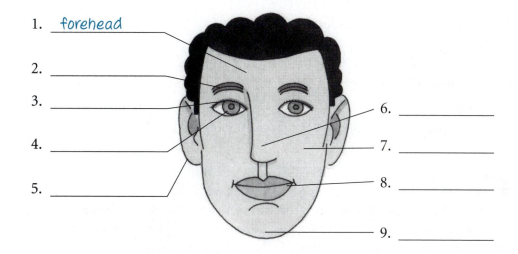

1. forehead

2. _____

3. _____

4. _____

5. _____

6. _____

7. _____

8. _____

9. _____

B   CD3 TRACK 3 **Listen and check your answers. Listen and repeat.**

Practice

PAIRS. **Student A, say a part of the body. Student B, point to the part of the
body in the picture and write the word. Take turns.**

Practice

A **Cross out the word that should not be in the group.**

1. eyes   eyelashes   eyebrows   ~~lips~~
2. ankle   knee   thigh   head   toe
3. shoulder   elbow   wrist   hand   eye
4. eyes   nose   breast   cheeks   lips
5. foot   ankle   toe   neck
6. thumb   finger   eyebrow   hand
7. buttocks   back   shoulders   ear
8. stomach   chin   eyes   head   ear

B **PAIRS.** **Check your answers. Give a reason.**

> **Example:**
>
> *I crossed out* lips. *The other words are parts of the eye.*

Make It Yours

Play "Simon Says." Everyone stands up. One person is the leader, "Simon." The leader will give commands. If the leader says *Simon Says,* follow the command. If the leader doesn't say *Simon Says,* don't follow the command.

> **Example:**
>
> *Simon says, Touch your eyebrow.* [Do this.]
> *Simon says, Touch your knee.* [Do this.]
> *Touch your hand.* [Don't do this!]

If the leader doesn't say *Simon Says,* and you follow the command, you must sit down.

Learn

 A *PAIRS.* **Complete the sentences with the words in the box.**

ankle	arm	~~back~~	foot	hand	hip

1. I hurt my _____ back _____.

2. I cut my _____.

3. I burned my _____.

4. I bruised my _____.

5. I sprained my _____.

6. I broke my _____.

 **B** **4** **Listen and check your answers. Listen and repeat.**

Practice

A **5** A patient is talking to her doctor. Listen to the conversation. Listen and repeat.

A: What's the matter?
B: I hurt my elbow.
A: When did it happen?
B: Yesterday.

B *PAIRS.* **Practice the conversation with other sentences from Learn. Change roles.**

Make It Yours

PAIRS. ROLE PLAY. **Student A, you are the doctor. Student B, you are the patient. Tell the doctor what's the matter. Take turns. Talk about something that really happened to you.**

BONUS *PAIRS.* **Complete the table with the parts of the body from Lesson 1. There are several correct answers.**

He sprained his . . .	He broke his . . .

Learn

A   What are the people saying? Write the sentences under the correct pictures.

I feel dizzy.	I have a rash.	I have a stiff neck.	~~I have an infection.~~
I feel nauseous.	I have a sore throat.	I have a stuffy nose.	My eyes are itchy.

1. ___I have an infection.___   2. _____   3. _____

4. _____   5. _____   6. _____

7. _____   8. _____

B    CD3 TRACK **6** Listen and check your answers. Listen and repeat.

Practice

A **Complete the sentences. Circle a, b, or c.**

1. I feel _____.
   - **a.** infection
   - **b.** nauseous
   - **c.** a stomachache

2. I have _____.
   - **a.** dizzy
   - **b.** itchy
   - **c.** an infection

3. My skin is _____.
   - **a.** itchy
   - **b.** rash
   - **c.** a fever

4. I have a _____ throat.
   - **a.** stiff
   - **b.** sore
   - **c.** stuffy

B *PAIRS.* **Check your answers.**

Make It Yours

A   **7** **A patient is talking to his doctor. Listen to the conversation. Listen and repeat.**

A: What's the matter?
B: I feel dizzy.
A: When did it start?
B: About two days ago.

B *PAIRS.* **Practice the conversation. Use the problems in Practice. Change roles.**

Learn

8 A patient is calling a medical clinic to make an appointment. Listen to the conversation. Listen and repeat.

A: Good morning. Watertown Family Practice. May I help you?
B: Yes. This is Rosa Mendez. I'd like to make an appointment.
A: What's the matter?
B: I have a cold and a fever.
A: When did the fever start?
B: Two days ago.
A: Can you come in tomorrow morning at 11:15?
B: Yes. That's fine.

Practice

A   Cover the conversation in Learn. Match the questions with the answers.

____c____ 1. May I help you?

_____ 2. What's the matter?

_____ 3. When did it start?

_____ 4. Can you come in this afternoon at 4:45?

a. I have a sore throat and a cough.

b. Yes, I can.

c. Yes, I'd like to make an appointment.

d. Yesterday.

B   *PAIRS.* Check your answers.

Make It Yours

PAIRS. ROLE PLAY. **Student A, you are the receptionist. Student B, you are the patient. Make an appointment for the patient to see the doctor. Change roles.**

Learn

A   **9** **Listen to the list of illnesses and conditions.**

1. cancer
2. diabetes
3. hypertension
4. TB (tuberculosis)
5. heart disease
6. asthma
7. high cholesterol
8. pneumonia
9. allergies
10. HIV (Human Immunodeficiency Virus)

B *PAIRS.* **Which words in Exercise A do you know? Tell your partner. Ask your teacher about words you don't know.**

C **Match the medical conditions with their descriptions.**

__b__ 1. asthma

____ 2. diabetes

____ 3. hypertension

____ 4. TB (tuberculosis)

____ 5. heart disease

____ 6. cancer

____ 7. high cholesterol

____ 8. HIV

____ 9. allergies

____ 10. pneumonia

a. an infection of the lungs

b. a condition that makes it difficult for a person to breathe

c. a disease that make a person's heart weak

d. too much sugar in the blood

e. high blood pressure

f. a virus that makes it impossible for the body to fight infections

g. a disease that makes tumors grow in the body

h. a bad reaction when eating, touching, or breathing certain things

i. a serious illness that affects the lungs and makes it hard for a person to breathe

j. too much fat in the blood

D *PAIRS.* **Check your answers.**

Note
> > > > >

Before you go visit the doctor, write a list of your medical conditions and your medical questions. A doctor's visit can be very short. It's easy to forget something!

Practice

A Read Thomas Lewis's medical history form. Circle *T* for *True* and *F* for *False*.

MG
Madison General
Medical History Form

Name Thomas Lewis   **Sex** male   **Date of Birth:** 9/20/85

Medical Conditions Do you have, or have you had any of the following? Answer "yes" or "no" for all questions. Explain your "yes" answers.	yes	no
asthma		X
HIV		X
cancer		X
diabetes It started in 2005. I take insulin daily.	X	
heart disease		X
pneumonia		X
high cholesterol		X
tuberculosis (TB)		X
hypertension		X
headaches		X
allergies I am allergic to penicillin and milk.	X	

1. Mr. Lewis has asthma.   T (F)

2. Mr. Lewis has diabetes.   T   F

3. Mr. Lewis takes medicine every day.   T   F

4. Mr. Lewis has high blood pressure.   T   F

5. Mr. Lewis is allergic to some medicines and foods.   T   F

6. Mr. Lewis gets a lot of headaches.   T   F

B *PAIRS.* **Check your answers.**

C Read the rest of Mr. Lewis's medical history form. Circle *T* for *True* and *F* for *False*.

---

1. Have you been under medical care in the last year? Explain. __I hurt my back two months ago. I have__ __physical therapy twice a week.__

2. Have you ever had a major surgery or operation? Explain. __No__

3. Have you been vaccinated for polio, diphtheria, and typhoid? When? __Yes, when I was a child.__

4. Do you have any physical condition that prevents you from doing strenuous work? Explain. __I can't lift__ __more than 20 pounds because of my back.__

5. Have you ever received care form a mental health professional? When? __Yes. I was depressed from__ __2001 to 2002. I was in therapy for two years.__

---

1. Mr. Lewis is under medical care now. (T) F

2. Mr. Lewis had the required vaccinations. T F

3. Mr. Lewis has a leg injury. T F

4. Mr. Lewis's injury prevents him from lifting heavy things. T F

5. Mr. Lewis has a mental health problem now. T F

D *PAIRS.* Check your answers.

Make It Yours

Go to page 197 to fill out your own medical history form.

BONUS *TEAMS.* What are other medical conditions? Make a list.

_____

_____

_____

Share your list with the class.

Learn

A Look at the pictures. Listen and point. Listen and repeat.

aspirin / tablets

acetaminophen / caplets

cough syrup / teaspoon (5 ml)

vitamin / capsules

antacid / tablespoon (15 ml)

cold medicine / geltabs

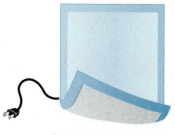

heating pad

ice pack

ointment

nasal spray

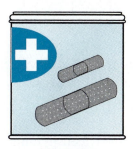

bandages

eye drops

B *PAIRS.* Look at the pictures in Exercise A. Check (✓) the things you have at home. Tell your partner.

> *Example:*
> *A: At home I have aspirin, cough syrup, . . .*

Practice

A **11** **Listen to the conversation. Listen and repeat.**

1. **A:** I have a headache. What should I do?
   B: You should <u>take</u> aspirin.

2. **A:** I burned my finger. What should I do?
   B: You should <u>put</u> ointment on it.

3. **A:** I have a stuffy nose. What should I do?
   B: You should <u>use</u> nasal spray.

4. **A:** I feel dizzy and I have a headache. What should I do?
   B: You should <u>see a doctor</u>!

B **Complete the table. Use words from Learn. Use each word only once.**

take	put _____ on it	use
aspirin	ointment	nasal spray

C *PAIRS.* **Check your answers.**

Make It Yours

PAIRS. **Make new conversations about medical problems.**

> *Example:*
>
> A: I bruised my leg. What should I do?
> B: You should put an ice pack on it and take aspirin.

BONUS *PAIRS.* **In your country what do you do for the following medical conditions? Tell your classmates.**

a sore throat	a burn
a cough	feeling nauseous
a fever	a bruise

Lesson 7 Medicine Labels

Learn

> **Note** >>>>> You can buy over-the-counter (OTC) medicine, like Ibuprofen, from any supermarket or drugstore. You don't need a prescription from the doctor.

A Read the medicine label. Match the words with their explanations.

_____ 1. allergy alert

_____ 2. temporary relief

_____ 3. expiration date

_____ 4. symptom

a. no pain for a little while

b. some people may be allergic to the medicine

c. condition that shows you may have a disease

d. don't take this medication after this date

Ibuprofen

Drug Facts

Active Ingredient: Ibuprofen 200 mg.

Uses: For the temporary relief of minor aches and pains due to the common cold, headache, toothache, backache. For the temporary relief of fever.

Warnings: Allergy alert: Ibuprofen may cause an allergic reaction. Symptoms may include rash and asthma.

Directions: Adults and children 12 years and older: Take one tablet every 4 to 6 hours. If pain or fever does not respond, 2 tablets may be used. Do not take more than 6 tablets in 24 hours.

Expiration date: 06/09

B Read the medicine label again. Circle *T* for *True* or *F* for *False*.

1. This medicine is for headaches.   (T)   F

2. This medicine is for asthma.   T   F

3. If you get a rash when you take this medicine, you are allergic to it.   T   F

4. This medicine is for children under 12.   T   F

5. It is OK to take 2 tablets every 4 hours for 24 hours.   T   F

6. Do not use this medicine after June 2009.   T   F

Learn

A Read the label. Then match the words with their definitions.

> ## Sav-Rite Pharmacy   Rx: 567989
>
> **Doctor:** Samuel Lummis   **Patient:** Barbara Moore
>
> **Dosage:** Take 1 tablet by mouth 2 times a day
> as needed for pain. Take with food.
>
> **Side effects:** May cause drowsiness.
> Use caution while driving.
>
> **Naproxen 500 mg**
>
> **2 Refills**   **Exp:** 12/05/09
>
> R_x

_c_ 1. dosage   a. the abbreviation for prescription

____ 2. drowsiness   b. more medicine

____ 3. refill   c. how much medicine to take

____ 4. as needed   d. when you need it

____ 5. side effects   e. the number on your prescription label

____ 6. prescription number   f. bad reactions some people have to the medicine

____ 7. Rx   g. sleepiness

B   **12** Listen and check your answers.

Listen

 13 Listen. What do you hear? Circle *a* or *b*.

1.   **a.** one teaspoon   **b.** one tablespoon

2.   **a.** two times a day   **b.** three times a day

3.   **a.** with food   **b.** without food

4.   **a.** drowsiness   **b.** dizziness

5.   **a.** Finish all the medicine.   **b.** Take it as needed.

6.   **a.** None.   **b.** One.

Practice

A   Read the medicine label in Learn. Answer the patient's questions. Circle *a* or *b*.

1. What's the name of the medicine?

    a. Dosage.   **(b.)** Naproxen.

2. How much should I take?

    a. Two times a day.   **b.** One tablet.

3. How often should I take it?

    a. Two times a day.   **b.** One tablet.

4. Should I take the medicine on an empty stomach?

    a. Yes.   **b.** No. It's not necessary.

5. What are its side effects?

    a. Drowsiness.   **b.** Caution.

6. Should I finish all the medicine?

    a. No. Take as needed.   **b.** Yes. Finish all the refills.

7. How many refills can I get?

    a. None.   **b.** Two.

8. Can I use this medicine in 2010?

    a. Yes.   **b.** No.

B   *PAIRS.* Check your answers.

Make It Yours

PAIRS. Look at the label. Write eight questions for the pharmacist.

1. _____

2. _____

3. _____

4. _____

5. _____

6. _____

7. _____

8. _____

RX: 222253
Wally's Pharmacy

Doctor: Alice Che   **Patient:** Jerry Mixer

Dosage: Take 1 tablet every 3 hours
             as needed for pain.
Take with food.
May cause dizziness.
May cause drowsiness.

Acetaminophen with Codeine

1 Refill   **Exp:** 03-08-10

Unit 9 Test

 Listening I [Tracks 14–17]

Listen to the sentence.
Which of the following means the same as the sentence
you heard: A, B, or C?

1. A. I don't have a headache.

B. I can't breathe easily.

C. I broke my toe.

2. A. His skin has red spots.

B. He cut himself.

C. He has a fever.

3. A. Fine, thanks.

B. What's the problem?

C. Where are you?

Listening II [Tracks 18–22]

**Listen to the first part of the conversation.
What should the person say next: A, B, or C?**

4. A. Today at school.

   B. I saw a doctor.

   C. On my elbow.

5. A. I saw a doctor.

   B. I feel nauseous.

   C. That's fine.

6. A. Take one tablet.

   B. My sink is leaking.

   C. I have a cough.

7. A. You should take aspirin.

   B. You should exercise.

   C. You should put ointment on it.

Reading

Read. What is the correct answer: A, B, C, or D?

Eastern Associates		Medical History Form		

Name	Sex	Date of Birth		
Mike Morgan	male	2/4/87		

Medical Conditions: Mark "Yes" or "No" for all medical conditions listed below. Explain "Yes" answers.

		Yes	No
headaches			X
allergies	I'm allergic to milk.	X	
heart disease			X
cancer			X
high cholesterol	since 1/4/03	X	

8. Which of Mike's medical conditions began in 2003?

    A. headaches

    B. allergies

    C. cancer

    D. high cholesterol

9. What is Mike allergic to?

    A. He's allergic to peanuts.

    B. He's allergic to milk.

    C. He's not allergic to anything.

    D. He's allergic to Ibuprofen.

Teri took her six-year-old daughter, Katie, to the park Saturday morning. Katie wanted to ride her bike there while her mom watched. It was a sunny day and the park was full of people playing soccer, having picnics, and enjoying the day.

Suddenly, a dog ran in front of Katie's bike as she came around a corner. Teri watched as her young daughter flew over the front of her bike and landed hard on her left shoulder. When Teri ran over, she saw that Katie's chin, eyebrow, and lips were bleeding. Teri and Katie left the park and went to their family clinic.

The doctor said that Katie had bruised her shoulder and sprained her wrist. He gave her children's pain medicine. The doctor told Teri that Katie needed a lot of rest. He asked Teri to make an appointment to come back on Friday.

10. What happened to Katie in the story?

    A. A dog fell while running in the park.

    B. Teri and Katie rode bikes in the park.

    C. Katie fell off her bike and got hurt.

    D. The doctor took Katie to the hospital.

11. What happened to Katie's wrist?

    A. She bruised it.

    B. She broke it.

    C. She rested it.

    D. She sprained it.

Allergy Medicine

Active Ingredients:
Diphenhydramine Hydrochloride

Uses: Temporarily relieves stuffy nose, itchy eyes

Warnings: Do not use with any other product containing diphenhydramine.

Directions:
Adults and children 12 years and over—
2 tablets every 4–6 hours, not to exceed
12 tablets in 24 hours.

Children 6 to under 12 years of age—1 tablet every 4–6 hours, not to exceed 8 tablets in 24 hours.

12. What does this medicine do?

A. It relieves allergy symptoms.

B. It is dangerous.

C. It causes nausea.

D. Take it as needed.

13. How often can an adult take this allergy medicine?

A. every 4 to 6 hours

B. every 12 hours

C. every 24 hours

D. every 8 hours

Unit 10 Safety Procedures

Lesson 1   **Safety Warnings**
- **Read labels on household products**
- **Learn how to call a poison control center**

Lesson 2   **Calling 911**
- **Learn how to call 911 to report an emergency**

Lesson 3   **Communicating with Police**
- **Learn how to respond to requests from a police officer**

Learn

> **Note**
> > > > >
> *Many household products have warning labels. The label may say POISON or DANGER or WARNING or CAUTION. If someone swallows, breathes in, or touches a dangerous product, call 800-222-1222. Call 911 if a person is unconscious or having convulsions.*

A **PAIRS.** Match the pictures to the directions.

a.

b.

c.

d.

e.

f.

_____ ⓑ 1. Avoid contact with eyes.

_____ 2. Avoid contact with skin.

_____ 3. Avoid breathing in vapors.

_____ 4. Avoid mixing with other liquids.

_____ 5. Keep out of reach of children.

_____ 6. Keep away from heat.

B CD3 TRACK 23 **Listen and check your answers.**

Practice

A   Read the labels. Ask your teacher about words you don't know.

B   Read the labels again and read the statements.
Write *T* for *True* or *F* for *False*.

Furniture Polish
CAUTION: CAUSES EYE IRRITAITON.

Avoid contact with eyes. In case of contact with eyes,
take out contact lenses, rinse immediately, and
continue flushing with water for about 15 minutes.
Get medical attention immediately.

__T__ 1. If you get furniture polish in your eyes,
you should rinse and flush out your eyes
with water.

Drain Cleaner
⚠ **DANGER** ⚠

Keep out of the reach of children and pets.
Can cause burns on contact. Harmful if swallowed.
If swallowed, do not induce vomiting. Rinse mouth immediately.
Drink a glass of water or milk. Then call poison control center,
physician, or emergency room.

_____ 2. If someone swallows drain cleaner, you
should make the person vomit.

BLEACH
WARNING: EYE AND SKIN IRRITANT.

Vapors may irritate. Harmful if swallowed.
Never use or mix with other household products.
Hazardous gases may result.
Use only in well-ventilated areas.
If breathing is affected, get fresh air immediately.

_____ 3. When you use bleach, you should close
the windows.

Insect spray (Aerosol Can)

CAUTION: △

Contents under pressure. Do not puncture or throw in fire.
Do not expose to heat or store at temperatures above 120°F.
Spray as directed.
Keep out of reach of children.

_____ 4. You should keep this insect spray in a
cool place.

Lighter Fluid
DANGER
Never add fluid to lighted fire.
Keep away from heat, sparks, and flames.
If swallowed, do not induce vomiting.
Call a doctor immediately.
Avoid breathing vapors. Avoid contact with skin.

_____ 5. You should spray lighter fluid on a
hot fire.

C   *PAIRS.* Check your answers.

Make It Yours

A   **Read the label. Ask your teacher about words you don't know.**

DANGER:

**KEEP OUT OF REACH OF
CHILDREN AND PETS.
CONTAINS UREA HYDROCHOLORIDE.
CAUSES EYE BURNS AND SKIN IRRITATION.**

Harmful if swallowed, inhaled, or absorbed
through the skin. Protective eyewear and
rubber gloves recommended. Do not get
in eyes or on skin or clothing. Do not mix
with bleach or other household chemicals
as toxic fumes may result.
Use in well-ventilated area.
FIRST AID: If in eyes: Hold eye open and
rinse slowly and gently with water for
15 minutes. Remove contact lenses.
Call a poison control center or doctor
immediately for treatment advice.
If on skin: Take off contaminated clothing.
Rinse skin immediately with plenty of water
for 15 minutes.
If swallowed: Drink a glass of water if able
to swallow. Do not induce vomiting.
If inhaled: Move to fresh air.
Storage/Disposal: Keep product in original
container at all times. Store on high shelf or
in locked cabinet and in a cool, dry place.
Do not reuse container.

B   **GROUPS OF 3. Answer the questions. Discuss.**

1. What should/shouldn't you do with this product?

2. What should you do if someone swallows it, touches it, or breathes it in?

3. What can you do to keep dangerous products away from children?

Learn

Note > > > > > *When you call a poison control center, a poison control specialist will answer the phone and ask the age and weight of the victim, what the victim took, how much he or she took, how he or she is feeling or acting right now, and your name and phone number.*

A   **24** **Listen to the telephone call. Listen and repeat.**

A: Poison Control Center.
B: I'm calling about my <u>daughter</u>. <u>She swallowed some furniture polish.</u>
A: How old is your <u>daughter</u>?
B: <u>Eight.</u>
A: How much does <u>she</u> weigh?
B: <u>Sixty pounds.</u>
A: Is <u>she</u> conscious?
B: Yes.
A: What's your name?
B: <u>Clara Charles.</u>
A: What's your telephone number?
B: <u>732-555-4250</u>.
A: Follow these directions.
B: OK.
A: . . .

B *PAIRS. ROLE PLAY.* **Call a poison control center. Use the words in the boxes and your own name and phone number.**

- son
- swallowed some floor cleaner fluid
- 6 years old
- 70 pounds

1.

- daughter
- sprayed glass cleaner in her eyes
- 12 years old
- 90 pounds

2.

- brother
- breathed in some tile cleaner vapors
- 45 years old
- 150 pounds

3.

- aunt
- got drain cleaner on her hand
- 32 years old
- 130 pounds

4.

Listen

 25 Listen to the conversations. What do you hear? Circle *a*, *b*, or *c*.

CONVERSATION 1

a.

b.

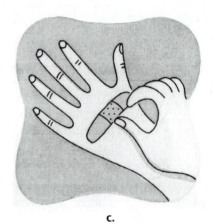

c.

CONVERSATION 2

a.

b.

c.

CONVERSATION 3

a.

b.

c.

BONUS **GROUPS OF 5.** Have you ever had an accident with a household product? What happened? What did you do?

152   Unit 10 Lesson 1

Learn

Note
> > > > >
Call 911 to report a crime, a fire, a car accident, or a medical emergency. Never call 911 when there is no emergency.

 26 **Listen and point to the emergencies. Listen and repeat.**

1. Someone is breaking into my neighbor's house.

2. There's a fight upstairs. It sounds violent.

3. My neighbor's house is on fire.

4. My husband is choking.

5. My purse was snatched.

6. I was mugged.

Practice

A **27** **Listen to the telephone call to 911. Listen and repeat.**

A: 911. What's the emergency?
B: <u>There was a car accident on my street.</u>
A: What's your name and address?
B: My name is <u>Sara Kim. I live at 42 Potter Road.</u>
A: . . .

B *PAIRS.* **Practice the conversation with other emergencies in the box. Use your own name and address.**

> Someone is breaking into my neighbor's house.
>
> There's a fight upstairs. It sounds violent.
>
> My neighbor's house is on fire.
>
> My husband is choking.
>
> My purse was snatched.
>
> I was mugged.

Make It Yours

PAIRS. **In what other situations would you call 911? Make a list.**

1. _____
2. _____
3. _____

BONUS *GROUPS OF 3.* **Discuss situations when you, someone in your family, or a friend had to call the police or 911. What happened?**

Learn

  Note > > > > >

If a police officer stops you when you are driving, do not get out of the car before the police officer tells you to. The officer will usually ask for your driver's license, car registration, and an insurance card. The officer will then tell you why he or she stopped you, or you can ask why you were stopped. It is OK to explain any special situations, but don't argue with the officer. You can explain your situation in court.

A 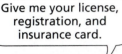 **28** **Listen to the police officer's commands. Listen and point.**

a. _____

b. _____

c. _____

d. _____

e. __1__

f. _____

g. _____

B **29** **Listen and number the pictures in the order you hear them.**

C *PAIRS.* **Check your answers.**

BONUS **With the class, discuss your experiences with traffic tickets or any other times you were stopped by the police.**

Unit 10 Test

 Listening I [Tracks 30–35]

Listen to the sentence.
Which of the following means the same as the sentence you heard: A, B, or C?

1. A. Do not mix with water.

   B. Avoid contact with eyes.

   C. Keep away from heat.

2. A. Open the window.

   B. Call the doctor now.

   C. Rinse skin with water.

3. A. Close the windows when you use the product.

   B. Keep children away from the windows.

   C. Don't breathe in the vapors.

4. A. I lost my purse.

   B. Someone took my purse.

   C. Someone broke my purse.

5. A. Is she awake?

   B. Is she nauseous?

   C. Is she breathing?

You will hear a conversation.
Then you will hear a question about the conversation.
What is the correct answer: A, B, or C?

6. A. The boy was mugged.

   B. The boy is choking.

   C. The boy is violent.

7. A. to say hello

   B. to give the man a ticket

   C. to see some identification

8. A. The neighbors are fighting.

   B. There's a fire next door.

   C. It's an emergency.

Reading

Read. What is the correct answer: A, B, C, or D?

> ## All-Purpose Cleaner
>
> **CAUTION:** Keep out of reach of children. Causes moderate eye irritation. Avoid contact with eyes. In case of contact with eyes, rinse immediately and continue flushing with water for about 15 minutes.

---

9. What can the cleaner do to your eyes?

    A. It can clean them.

    B. It can hurt them.

    C. It can rinse them.

    D. It can flush out the water.

10. What should you do if the cleaner gets in your eyes?

    A. Cause irritation in your eyes.

    B. Avoid contact with your eyes.

    C. Rinse your eyes with water.

    D. Close your eyes.

Pro Glass Cleaner

DANGER

KEEP OUT OF REACH OF CHILDREN.
IF SWALLOWED, DRINK A GLASS OF
WATER AND CALL A PHYSICIAN
IMMEDIATELY. IN CASE OF EYE CONTACT,
RINSE THOROUGHLY WITH WATER.

Made in the USA.

---

11. What should you do if you swallow this glass cleaner?

    A. Call a doctor.

    B. Rinse your eyes.

    C. Keep out of reach of children.

    D. Go to the hospital.

12. Who should not use this glass cleaner?

    A. physicians

    B. children

    C. Pro Glass professional cleaners

    D. people with glasses

Poison Control Center   1-800-222-1222

Did you swallow a chemical?
   Drink a small amount of milk or water.
   Call **1-800-222-1222**.

Did you breathe in a poison?
   Get to fresh air and call **1-800-222-1222**.

Did poison get on your skin?
   Take off any clothing that the poison touched.
   Rinse skin with running water for 15–20 minutes.
   Call **1-800-222-1222**.

Did poison get in your eyes?
   Rinse eyes with running water for 15–20 minutes.
   Call **1-800-222-1222**.

---

13. What should you do if you get poison on your skin?

   A. Get fresh air.

   B. Drink a small amount of milk.

   C. Rinse your eyes.

   D. Rinse your skin with water.

14. What should you do if you swallow a chemical?

   A. Take off any clothing with poison on it.

   B. Drink a little milk or water.

   C. Run water for 15 to 20 minutes.

   D. Call the doctor the next day.

Unit 11 Getting a Job

Lesson 1   **Help Wanted Ads**
- **Read ads that include abbreviations**

Lesson 2   **Job Application 1**
- **Fill out a job application form**

Lesson 3   **Job Application 2**
- **Put events in chronological order**

Lesson 4   **A Job Interview**
- **Respond appropriately to job interview questions**
- **Practice appropriate job interview behavior**

Learn

PAIRS. Look at the two job ads. What do the underlined words mean?

> **Example:**
> A: _Part-time_ means you don't work 40 hours a week.
> B: That's right. _Experience required_ means that you did the job before.

COOK

<u>Part-time</u>, weekends,
<u>experience required</u>,
$12/hour,
<u>apply in person</u>.
Bistro Restaurant
3132 West 6ᵗʰ Street
Los Angeles

Administrative Assistant

<u>Full-time</u>, Monday to Friday,
$10/hr, <u>excellent benefits</u>,
<u>references required</u>.
State Insurance Agency
Call 213-555-9621

Practice

 A **PAIRS.** Student A, look at the ad for the cook. Student B, cover the ad for the cook. Ask Student A the questions and write the answers.

1. What's the job? _____

2. Is the job full-time or part-time? _____

3. How much is the pay? _____

4. What are the hours? _____

5. Are there benefits? _____

6. What's the name of the company? _____

7. How do you apply for the job? _____

B **PAIRS.** Student B, look at the ad for the administrative assistant. Student A, cover the ad for the administrative assistant. Ask Student B the questions in Exercise A and write the answers.

Learn

 A   Read the ads. Look at the words. Write the abbreviations.

> ### Sales Clerk
> PT, wknds, eves, exp. req.
> $9/hr. apply in prsn.
> Bay Department Store
> 213-555-6321

> ### BUS DRIVER
> FT, M–F., exp. req.
> $18/hr. exc. bens.,
> refs. req.,
> Metro Bus Company
> 626-555-3604

1. experience required _exp. req._
2. full-time _____
3. weekends _____
4. per hour _____
5. part-time _____

6. apply in person _____
7. Monday to Friday _____
8. evenings _____
9. excellent benefits _____
10. references required _____

 B   *PAIRS.* Check your answers.

Practice

PAIRS. Look at the ads. Take turns asking and answering the questions.

> ### NURSE
> **F/T**
> **Monday–Friday**
> **$18.50/hr.**
> **gd. bens.**

> ### Office Worker
> P/T some wknds,
> $8.50/hr. no bens.
> Acme Electric
> Call Joe at 809-555-8765,
> M–F 9–5

1. Which job is full-time? _____
2. Which job pays better? _____
3. Which job has benefits? _____
4. Which job is part-time? _____
5. Which job requires weekend hours? _____

Listen

  Listen. What do you hear? Circle the words.

1. Jose works **full-time / part-time**.

2. The pay is **$8.00 an hour / $18.00 an hour**.

3. **Experience / No experience** is necessary.

4. You'll be working **weekends / weekdays**.

5. **The benefits / The hours** are excellent.

6. **References are / Experience is** required.

Make It Yours

A **Write an ad for a job you want. Use abbreviations.**

B *PAIRS.* **Look at your partner's ad. Do you want to apply for this job? Explain your answer.**

BONUS *GROUPS OF 3.* **Tell your group about the job you have now or had in the past. Explain which days you work, whether you work full-time or part-time, what the benefits are, and whether experience is required. Add any other details.**

Learn

 41 John Hall is filling out an employment application. Look at the first part of the application. Listen and point to the words.

SAMMY'S
EMPLOYMENT APPLICATION

PERSONAL INFORMATION

NAME ___John___   ___M.___   ___Hall___   PHONE ___310-555-2167___
    First Middle Last

ADDRESS ___1500 Sawmill Boulevard___   ___Los Angeles___   ___CA___   ___98765___
     Street   City   State Zip Code

Are you older than 18? Yes ☒ No ☐

AVAILABLITY

When can you begin work? ___July___   ___1___   ___2007___
          Month Day Year

Are you interested in full-time? ___✓___   Part-time? _____

Can you work overtime? Yes ☒ No ☐

Hours Available	Sunday	Monday	Tuesday	Wednesday	Thursday	Friday	Saturday
FROM	2:00 P.M.	2:00 P.M.	2:00 P.M.	2:00 P.M.	2:00 P.M.	2:00 P.M.	2:00 P.M.
TO	9:00 P.M.	9:00 P.M.	9:00 P.M.	9:00 P.M.	9:00 P.M.	9:00 P.M.	9:00 P.M.

Are you legally able to work in the U.S.? Yes ☒ No ☐

Do you have transportation to work? Yes ☒ No ☐

Practice

 A Look at the employment application in Learn. Fill in the information.

1. Is John over the age of 18? _____.

2. John can begin work on _____.

3. He is available to work from _____ to _____.
            day   day

4. He is available to work from _____ to _____.
            time   time

5. Can he work extra hours? _____.

6. Is he legally able to work in the United States? _____.

7. Does he have transportation to work? _____.

B   *PAIRS.* Check your answers.

Make It Yours

A You want to work at Sammy's. Complete the application. (It's OK to use made-up information when you fill out the form.)

SAMMY'S
EMPLOYMENT APPLICATION

PERSONAL INFORMATION

NAME _____ PHONE _____

First　　　　　　Middle　　　　　　Last

ADDRESS _____

Street　　　　　　　　City　　　　　　State　　　　　Zip Code

Are you older than 18? Yes ☐ No ☐

AVAILABLITY

When can you begin work? _____

Month　　　　　　Day　　　　　　Year

Are you interested in full-time? _____ Part-time? _____

Can you work overtime? Yes ☐ No ☐

Hours Available	Sunday	Monday	Tuesday	Wednesday	Thursday	Friday	Saturday
FROM							
TO							

Are you legally able to work in the U.S.? Yes ☐ No ☐

Do you have transportation to work? Yes ☐ No ☐

B *PAIRS.* Check your partner's employment application form. Is it complete? Is it written clearly?

Note >>>>> *On a job application form, it is not legal for an employer to ask about an applicant's age, date of birth, sex, race, skin color, national origin, religion, number of children, or physical disability. In most states, the employer cannot ask about marital status.*

Bonus *PAIRS.* Tell your partner about an experience you had applying for a job. If you haven't applied for a job, talk about someone you know.

Learn

 John Hall is filling out the other sections of the employment form. Look at the form. Listen and point to the words.

MOST RECENT EDUCATION:

Name __Jefferson High School__   Street Address __5432 South Washington Boulevard__

City __Los Angeles__   State __CA__   Zip Code __98765__   Phone Number __310-555-1679__

Teacher or Counselor __Ms. Simmons__   Department __English__   Last Grade Completed __12__

Now Enrolled? Yes ☐ No ☒   Graduated? Yes ☒ No ☐   School Sports or Activities __baseball__

WORK HISTORY: (List your two most recent jobs.)

1. Company __The Grill__ Address __2003 Beverly Boulevard__ City __Los Angeles__ State __CA__ Zip __91234__

   Area Code __323__   Phone Number __555-1234__   Job __waiter__

   Supervisor __Martha James__   Dates Worked: From __2/05__   To __present__

   Salary __$7.00 hr.__   Reason for Leaving __looking for a better job__

2. Company __Pat's Cafe__ Address __8400 W. Sunrise Blvd.__ City __West Hollywood__ State __CA__ Zip __95432__

   Area Code __323__   Phone Number __555-8585__   Job __bus person__

   Supervisor __Pat__   Dates Worked: From __6/03__   To __2/05__

   Salary __$6.00/hr.__   Reason for Leaving __restaurant closed__

MILITARY HISTORY:
Have you served in the U.S. Military? Yes ☐ No ☒

Practice

A   **Look at the employment application in Learn. Fill in the information.**

1. Did John graduate from high school? _____

2. What was John's most recent job? _____

3. Where did John most recently work? _____

4. Is he still working there? _____

5. What was John's job in 2004? _____

B   *PAIRS.* **Check your answers.**

C   *PAIRS.* **Look at Carol Chu's work history. Answer the questions.**

• Secretary at Transnational Insurance Company from 6/03 to present.
• File Clerk at Berkeley and Berkeley from 7/99 to 8/01.
• Receptionist at Dr. Lansing's office from 8/01 to 6/03.

1. Which job should she write first on the application? _____

2. Which job should she write next? _____

Make It Yours

A   **Write your information on the form. (It's OK to use made-up information when you fill out the form.)**

MOST RECENT EDUCATION:

Name _____   Street Address _____

City _____   State _____   Zip Code _____   Phone Number _____

Teacher or Counselor _____   Department _____   Last Grade Completed _____

Now Enrolled? Yes ☐ No ☐   Graduated? Yes ☐ No ☐   School Sports or Activities _____

WORK HISTORY: (List your two most recent jobs.)

1. Company _____   Address _____   City _____   State _____ Zip _____

   Area Code _____   Phone Number _____   Job _____

   Supervisor _____   Dates Worked: From _____   To _____

   Salary _____   Reason for Leaving _____

2. Company _____   Address _____   City _____   State _____ Zip _____

   Area Code _____   Phone Number _____   Job _____

   Supervisor _____   Dates Worked: From _____   To _____

   Salary _____   Reason for Leaving _____

MILITARY HISTORY:
Have you served in the U.S. Military? Yes ☐ No ☐

B   *PAIRS.* **Check your partner's employment application form. Is it complete? Is it written clearly?**

BONUS   **Fill out the employment application on page 199.**

Learn

Note
> > > > >

When you are interviewing for a job, it is important to:
- *wear appropriate clothing.*
- *shake hands and smile when you meet.*
- *make eye contact.*

If the interviewer asks, Can you _____? *and you can't, answer,* No, I can't. But I can learn.

A   **Sonia Martinez is interviewing for a job. Listen to your teacher. Listen and repeat.**

A: I see you're applying for the <u>office worker</u> job. Can you <u>use a computer</u>?
B: Yes, I can.

B   *PAIRS.* **Practice the conversation.**

Practice

A   **Match the questions with the jobs. There may be more than one correct answer.**

<u> c </u> 1. Can you operate a forklift?   a. office worker

_____ 2. Can you use a lawnmower?   b. hairdresser

_____ 3. Can you make an omelet?   c. factory worker

_____ 4. Can you use a computer?   d. gardener

_____ 5. Do you have a license?   e. cook

B   *PAIRS.* **Write new conversations. Use the conversation in Learn and talk about other jobs.**

C   *PAIRS.* **Practice your conversations. Take turns.**

Make It Yours

A   *PAIRS.* **Choose a job you want. Use the jobs in Practice or your own ideas. Write a new conversation for each job.**

B   *PAIRS.* **Role-play your conversations. Remember to make eye contact. (It's OK to use made-up information for the role plays.) Take turns.**

Unit 11 Test

Listening I [Tracks 43–45]

Listen to the first part of the conversation.
What should the person say next: A, B, or C?

1. A. Can you work the night shift?

   B. OK, when can you start?

   C. Are there benefits?

2. A. Do you have references?

   B. Can you drive?

   C. Can you make an omelet?

Listening II [Tracks 46–49]

Listen. Everything is on the audio CD.

Reading

Read. What is the correct answer: A, B, C, or D?

Super Dry Cleaners
Employment Application

PERSONAL INFORMATION

NAME ___Maria___ ___J.___ ___Herrera___   PHONE ___713-555-0023___
First   Middle   Last

ADDRESS ___112 Granada Ave.___ ___Mission Viejo___ ___CA___ ___92961___
Street   City   State   Zip Code

Are you older than 18? ___X___ Yes _____ No

AVAILABLITIY

When can you begin work? ___June 10, 2007___

Hours available

	Monday	Tuesday	Wednesday	Thursday	Friday	Saturday	Sunday
From	9 A.M.	9 A.M.	9 A.M.	9 A.M.	9 A.M.	X	X
To	1 P.M.	1 P.M.	1 P.M.	1 P.M.	1 P.M.	X	X

6. Is Maria available to work on the weekend?

   A. Yes, she is.

   B. She can work Saturday.

   C. No, she isn't.

   D. She can begin June 10.

7. When can Maria start work at Super Dry Cleaners?

   A. on Monday at 9:00

   B. on weekends

   C. on Thursday until 1:00

   D. on June 10

Super Dry Cleaners
Employment Application

WORK HISTORY (List your two most recent jobs.)

1. Company **Alex's Dry Cleaners**
   Street Address **23452 Santos Street**   Phone **555-0989**
   City **Aliso Viejo**   State **CA**   Zip Code **92233**
   Job **cashier/clerk**   Supervisor **Karen White**
   Dates worked **1/05–present**   Salary **$7.00 hr.**
   Reason for leaving **Need more money**

2. Company **El Pollo Grill**
   Street Address **6678 N. Harbor Blvd.**   Phone **555-0988**
   City **Santa Ana**   State **CA**   Zip Code **92213**
   Job **cashier**   Supervisor **Hoa Lam**
   Dates worked **2/02–12/04**   Salary **$6.45 hr.**
   Reason for leaving **Restaurant closed**

---

8. What is Maria's job now?

   A. She is a cashier/clerk.

   B. She is a cook.

   C. She started work in 2002.

   D. The restaurant closed.

9. When did Maria start her job at El Pollo Grill?

   A. May 2005

   B. February 2002

   C. January 2005

   D. December 2004

10. How does a person apply for this job?

    A. References required.

    B. Call on the phone.

    C. Apply in person.

    D. Apply online.

11. What is required for this job?

    A. a car

    B. Monday to Friday

    C. references and experience

    D. $10.80 an hour and benefits

Unit 12 On the Job

Lesson 1   **Pay Day**
- **Read a paycheck stub**

Lesson 2   **An Employee Accident Form**
- **Fill out an employee accident report**

Lesson 3   **A Work Schedule**
- **Read and talk about a work schedule**

Lesson 4   **Computers**
- **Identify the parts of a computer**

Learn

A   **50** Look at the pay stub. Listen and point. Listen and repeat.

Jiffy Window Coverings

Name	Chen, Michael		Employee Number	9587	Hourly Pay	$ 10.00
Social Security Number	123-45-6789				Net Pay	$771.08
Pay Period	June 2–June 15, 2007					

Pay Type	Hours	Amount	Deductions	Amount
Regular	80	800.00	FICA	30.40
			Federal Withholding	107.05
Overtime	10	150.00	State Withholding	24.70
			SDI	16.77
Total Gross Pay		$950.00	**Total Deductions**	178.92

B Match the words with their definitions.

1. _c_ gross pay
2. ___ net pay
3. ___ regular pay
4. ___ overtime pay
5. ___ pay period
6. ___ hourly pay
7. ___ FICA
8. ___ Federal Withholding Tax
9. ___ State Withholding Tax
10. ___ SDI

a. amount after deductions are taken out

b. amount you earned per hour

c. amount you earned before taxes

d. extra pay for more than 40 hours of work in a week

e. income tax taken by the U.S. government

f. pay for 40 hours worked in a week

g. time covered by this paycheck

h. State Disability Insurance: money taken for medical care if you can't work because of an injury or illness not related to your job

i. Federal Insurance Contributions Act: Social Security retirement benefits

j. income tax taken by the state government

C *PAIRS.* Check your answers.

Practice

A Look at the pay stub in Learn. Answer the questions.

1. What is Mr. Chen's regular pay per hour? _____ $10.00 _____

2. What is Mr. Chen's pay for 1 hour of overtime? _____

3. How many hours did Mr. Chen work? _____

4. When did the pay period begin? _____

5. When did the pay period end? _____

6. How much money did Mr. Chen earn before taxes? _____

7. How much money did Mr. Chen take home? _____

8. How much was deducted for Social Security? _____

9. How much income was deducted for federal taxes? _____

10. How much income was deducted for state taxes? _____

11. How much was deducted for State Disability Insurance? _____

B *PAIRS.* Check your answers.

Note
> > > > >

Minimum Wage
Federal Minimum Wage is the lowest pay per hour that an employer is allowed to pay.

Overtime Pay
Overtime is working more than 40 hours a week.
Overtime pay is usually 1 ½ times (time and a half) regular pay.

Example:
I work 52 hours a week.
My pay is $10.00 an hour for 40 hours.
My pay is $15.00 an hour for 12 hours of overtime.
My gross pay is $580.00 per week.

BONUS *PAIRS.* Discuss. What is your dream job? How much net pay would you get every two weeks?

Learn

A Mark Perry is an employee at Philips Parts Warehouse. Read the paragraph. What's the paragraph about?

> Mark Perry has been working in the shipping department at Philips Parts Warehouse for the last two years. Yesterday morning at around 10 A.M., he was on the loading dock, loading boxes on a truck. He slipped and fell. He hurt his knee. The doctor said his knee was sprained. The doctor gave him some medicine for the pain and told him to return to work in two days.

B *PAIRS.* Answer the questions about Mr. Perry.

1. How long has Mr. Perry been working at Philips Parts Warehouse? _____

2. What department does he work in? _____

3. What happened to him? _____

4. What part of his body did he injure? _____

5. When did it happen? _____

6. What did the doctor give Mr. Perry? _____

C *PAIRS.* Check your answers. Read the paragraph again.

Note
>>>>>

If you have an accident at work, report the accident to your employer immediately.
If you are in pain, ask for medical care. Fill out an accident report as soon as possible
after a work accident occurs.

Practice

A   Imagine that you are Mark Perry. Look at the employee accident
report. Use the information in the paragraph in Learn to fill it out. Use
yesterday's date for the date of the accident and today's date for the
date of the report.

Philips Parts
Employee Accident Report

Name _____   Department _____

Date of Accident _____   Time _____

Location _____

Description of Accident _____
_____

Part of Body Injured _____

Type of Injury _____

Did the injured employee receive medical attention? _____

Has the employee returned to work? _____

If no, expected date of return _____

Employee Signature *Mark Perry* _____

Date of Report _____

B   *PAIRS.* Check your answers.

BONUS   *PAIRS.* Have you ever had an accident at work or at home? Tell your
partner what happened. Were you hurt? Did you go to the doctor?
Fill out the accident report on page 201.

Learn

A   **Match the information.**

  __b__   1. full-time   a. 8:00 A.M.–4:00 P.M.

  _____ 2. part-time   b. 40 hours a week

  _____ 3. day shift   c. 2:00 P.M.–10:00 P.M.

  _____ 4. afternoon shift   d. less than 40 hours a week

  _____ 5. night shift   e. day with no work

  _____ 6. lunch hour   f. time off to eat

  _____ 7. day off   g. 10:00 P.M.–6:00 A.M.

B   *PAIRS.* **Check your answers.**

C   **51**   **Look at Brenda Miller's work schedule. Listen and point.**

Capital Cleaning Supply Company

Work Schedule for Brenda Miller

Mon.	Tues.	Wed.	Thurs.	Fri.	Sat.
off	7:00 A.M.–3:00 P.M.	7:00 A.M.–3:00 P.M.	7:00 A.M..–3:00 P.M.	7:00 A.M.–3:00 P.M.	7:00 A.M.–3:00 P.M.
	lunch 11:00 A.M.–12:00 P.M.	lunch 11:00 A.M.–12:00 P.M.	lunch 11:00 A.M.–12:00 P.M.	lunch 11:00 A.M.–12:00 P.M.	lunch 11:00 A.M.–12:00 P.M.

*** All workers: Take a one-hour lunch in the middle of your work shift.

D   **Read the work schedule again. Fill in the information.**

1. Brenda's days off are _____ and _____.

2. Her lunch hour is from _____ to _____.

3. She works the _____ shift.

4. Brenda works _____ time, _____ hours a week.

5. Brenda takes _____ hour for lunch.

E   *PAIRS.* **Check your answers.**

Practice

 Note
>>>>> *Full-time is 40 hours a week. Lunch time is included in the 40 hours.*

A Look at the work schedule. Read the sentences. Circle *T* for *True* or *F* for *False.* Correct the false answers.

Capital Cleaning Supply Company

Work Schedule for the Week of _____ November 13 _____

Name	Mon.	Tues.	Wed.	Thurs.	Fri.	Sat.
Brenda Miller		7:00 A.M.–3:00 P.M.	7:00 A.M.–3:00 P.M.	7:00 A.M.–3:00 P.M.	7:00 A.M.–3:00 P.M.	7:00 A.M.–3:00 P.M.
Dinh Pham	2:00–10:00 P.M.	2:00–10:00 P.M.				2:00–10:00 P.M.
Alex Bennett	9:00 A.M.–5:00 P.M.	9:00 A.M.–5:00 P.M.	9:00 A.M.–5:00 P.M.		9:00 A.M.–5:00 P.M.	9:00 A.M.–5:00 P.M.
Verne Silvain	10:00 A.M.–6:00 P.M.			10:00 A.M.–6:00 P.M.	10:00 A.M.–6:00 P.M.	
Maria Rivera	2:00–10:00 P.M.	2:00–10:00 P.M.	2:00–10:00 P.M.			2:00–10:00 P.M.

*** All workers: Take a one-hour lunch in the middle of your work shift.**

1. Brenda works full-time.   (T) F
2. Dinh's days off are Friday and Monday.   T   F
3. Dinh works part-time.   T   F
4. Maria works the afternoon shift.   T   F
5. Alex works the night shift.   T   F
6. Verne works from 7 A.M. to 4 P.M.   T   F
7. Maria's days off are Thursday and Friday.   T   F
8. Alex works full-time.   T   F

B *PAIRS.* Check your answers.

Make It Yours

A   *PAIRS.* Interview your partner. Write the answers. (If you do not work, use your imagination.)

1. Do you work full-time or part-time? _____

2. What days do you work? _____

3. What are your days off? _____

4. Do you work the day shift, afternoon shift, or night shift? _____

5. What hours do you work? _____

6. Do you take a lunch or dinner break? When? How long is your lunch or dinner break? _____

B   Fill in the work schedule with your partner's information.

Work Schedule for _____   Week of _____
                                (name)   (dates)

Sunday	Monday	Tuesday	Wednesday	Thursday	Friday	Saturday

C   *PAIRS.* Show the work schedule to your partner. Is it correct?

BONUS   Interview someone outside of class. Fill in the person's work schedule below. Show it to the class.

Work Schedule for _____   Week of _____
                            (name)   (dates)

Sunday	Monday	Tuesday	Wednesday	Thursday	Friday	Saturday

Learn

 **52** **Listen and point. Listen and repeat.**

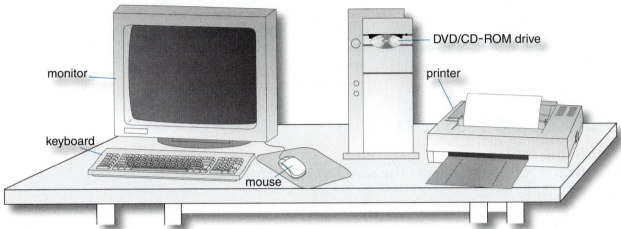

monitor

keyboard

mouse

DVD/CD-ROM drive

printer

Practice

Read the paragraph. Then match the words to their definitions.

Clara uses her computer for her schoolwork. She likes to use the **word processing program** to type her writing assignments because she can easily make changes. With word processing, she can **delete** and **insert** words. She can also move sentences and paragraphs without retyping by **cutting and pasting**. When she finishes the writing assignment, she can **print** it and save it in a **computer file**. Later, she can open the file and continue her work. Clara also uses the **Internet**. She **e-mails** her friends. She also does **research** for school.

_c_ 1. word processing program

___ 2. delete

___ 3. insert

___ 4. cut and paste

___ 5. print

___ 6. computer file

___ 7. Internet

___ 8. e-mail

___ 9. research

a. use a machine to copy documents and other computer files onto paper

b. a computer network that allows people around the world to exchange information

c. a computer program used for writing letters, reports, etc.

d. the activity of finding information about something

e. remove a letter, word, etc., from a document

f. send and receive messages by computer

g. add something to a document

h. information that is stored on a computer

i. take a part of a document and move it to another place in that or another document

Unit 12 Test

 Listening I [Tracks 53–56]

Listen to the sentence.
Which of the following means the same as the sentence you heard: A, B, or C?

1. A. He doesn't work part-time.

   B. He works nights from 6 to 10 P.M.

   C. He doesn't work on Saturday or Sunday.

2. A. She works the day shift.

   B. She works the night shift.

   C. She works part-time.

3. A. I need to print a letter.

   B. I use the Internet to write to people.

   C. I help my friends with their homework.

 Listening II [Tracks 57–61]

Listen. Everything is on the audio CD.

Reading

Read. What is the correct answer: A, B, C, or D?

Thomas works for the Delicious Food Company. He cuts sandwich meat on a large cutting machine. Thomas has worked for Delicious Foods for eleven years, and he really likes his job.

Last month he had an accident at work. He was cutting roast beef when his hand slipped, and two fingers on his right hand were badly cut in the machine. A co-worker took Thomas to the hospital. The doctors operated on his hand, and they saved his fingers.

Thomas's manager, Jorge, helped Thomas fill out an accident report. Jorge told Thomas not to worry about the medical bills, because the Delicious Food Company had insurance to pay for accidents. Thomas can return to work as soon as he is ready.

8. How long has Thomas worked for the company?

    A. two years

    B. eleven years

    C. one month

    D. two months

9. What will Thomas write on the accident report to describe what happened?

    A. I slipped and fell while I was working.

    B. I cut two fingers badly in the cutting machine.

    C. I hurt my hand when I fell at work.

    D. I want to come back to work but I can't.

10. Who will pay the hospital bills?

    A. Thomas

    B. his boss

    C. the doctors

    D. the insurance company

Delicious
Foods Company _____

Work Schedule for Thomas Soto

Sunday	Monday	Tuesday	Wednesday	Thursday	Friday	Saturday
OFF	7 A.M.–3 P.M.	7 A.M.–3 P.M.	7 A.M.–3 P.M.	7 A.M.–3 P.M.	7 A.M.–3 P.M.	OFF

All workers need to take a one-hour lunch or dinner break in the middle of their work shift.

11. Which days does Thomas have off?

   A. He is off weekdays.

   B. He works the day shift.

   C. He's off on weekends.

   D. He works full-time.

12. How much time do employees at Delicious Foods get for a meal break?

   A. 1 hour

   B. 1½ hours

   C. 45 minutes

   D. 2 hours

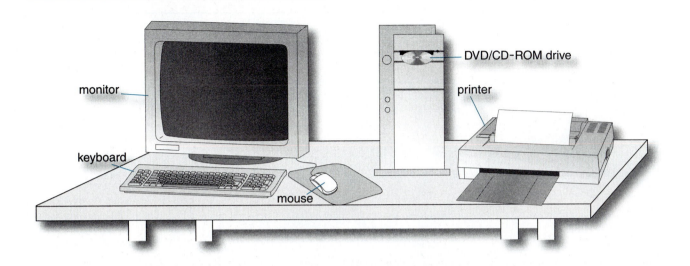

monitor

keyboard

mouse

DVD/CD-ROM drive

printer

13. Which part of the computer do you type on?

    A. the mouse

    B. the keyboard

    C. the printer

    D. the monitor

14. Which part of the computer makes a paper copy of the work?

    A. the printer

    B. the keyboard

    C. the mouse

    D. the monitor

15. What do we call messages we send through the Internet?

    A. e-mail

    B. a file

    C. a word-processing program

    D. a DVD/CD-ROM

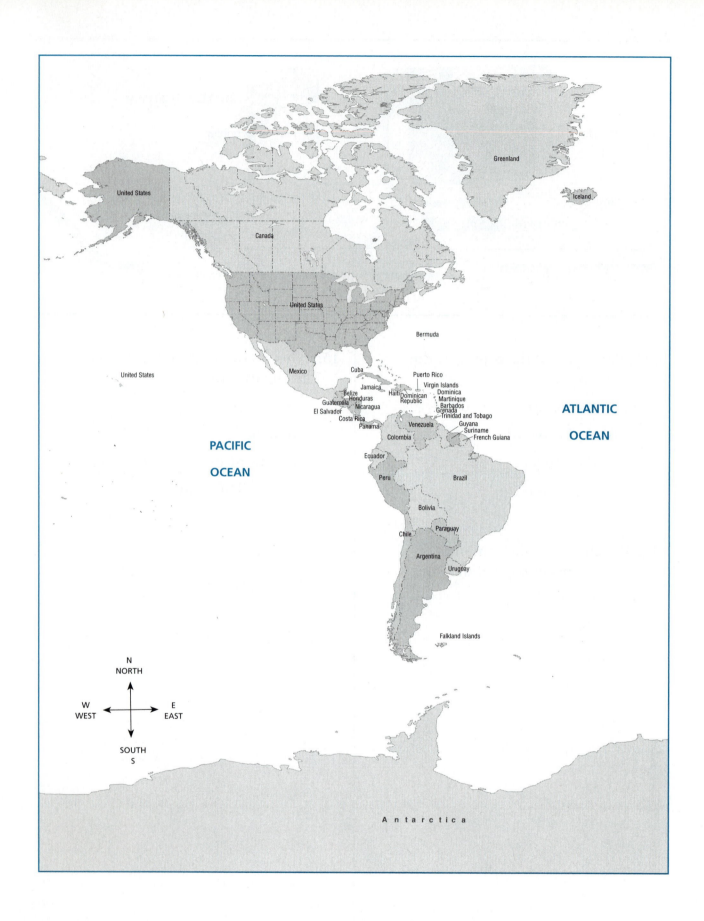

Greenland

Iceland

United States

Canada

United States

BERMUDA

United States

Mexico

Cuba

Puerto Rico

Virgin Islands

Jamaica

Belize

Honduras

Haiti

Dominican
Republic

Dominica

Martinique

Barbados

Guatemala

Nicaragua

Grenada

El Salvador

Costa Rica

Trinidad and Tobago

Panama

Venezuela

Guyana

Suriname

Colombia

French Guiana

ATLANTIC
OCEAN

PACIFIC
OCEAN

Ecuador

Peru

Brazil

Bolivia

Chile

Paraguay

Argentina

Uruguay

Falkland Islands

N
NORTH

W
WEST

E
EAST

SOUTH
S

A n t a r c t i c a

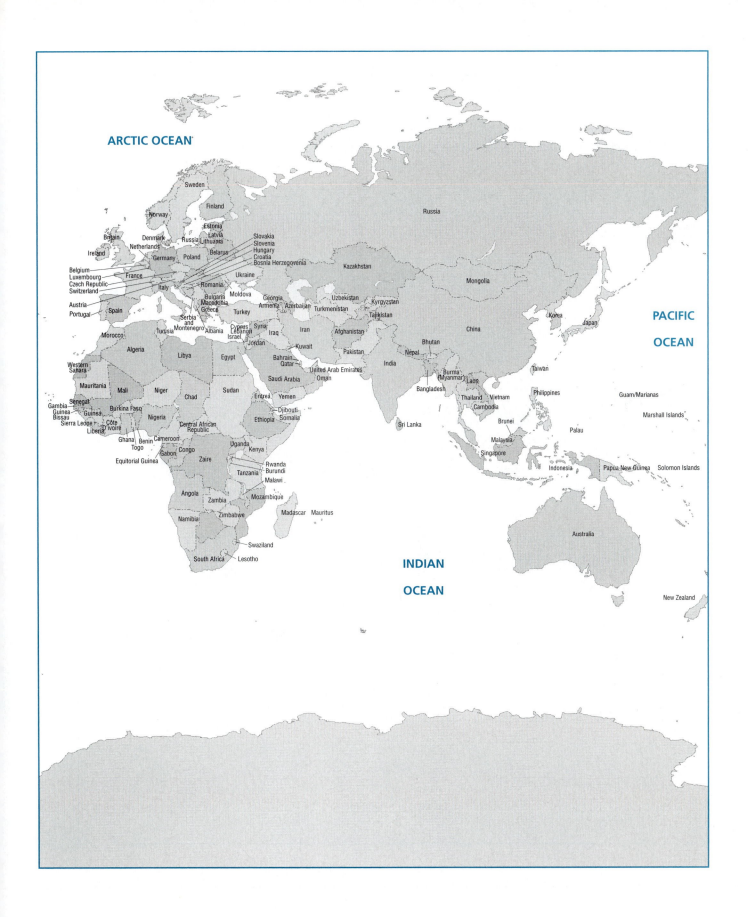

ARCTIC OCEAN

Sweden

Norway

Finland

Russia

Britain

Denmark

Estonia
Latvia
Lithuania

Slovakia
Slovenia
Hungary
Croatia
Bosnia Herzegovenia

Ireland

Netherlands

Russia

Belarus

Germany

Poland

Kazakhstan

Mongolia

Belgium
Luxembourg
Czech Republic
Switzerland

France

Ukraine

Italy

Romania

Austria

Portugal

Spain

Bulgaria
Macedonia
Greece

Moldova

Georgia
Armenia

Azerbaijan

Uzbekistan

Kyrgyzstan

Turkey

Turkmenistan

Tajikistan

Korea

Japan

PACIFIC

OCEAN

Serbia
and
Montenegro

Albania

Cyprus
Lebanon
Israel

Syria

Jordan

Iraq

Iran

Afghanistan

China

Morocco

Tunisia

Bhutan

Algeria

Libya

Egypt

Kuwait

Bahrain
Qatar

United Arab Emirates

Oman

Pakistan

Nepal

Burma
(Myanmar)

Laos

Taiwan

Western
Sahara

Saudi Arabia

India

Bangladesh

Thailand

Vietnam

Philippines

Guam/Marianas

Mauritania

Mali

Niger

Chad

Sudan

Eritrea

Yemen

Cambodia

Marshall Islands

Gambia
Guinea
Bissau

Senegal

Guinea

Burkina Faso

Djibouti

Somalia

Brunei

Palau

Sierra Leone

Côte
D'ivoire

Nigeria

Central African
Republic

Ethiopia

Sri Lanka

Malaysia

Liberia

Ghana

Benin

Cameroon

Singapore

Togo

Gabon

Congo

Uganda

Kenya

Indonesia

Papua New Guinea

Solomon Islands

Equitorial Guinea

Zaire

Rwanda
Burundi

Tanzania

Malawi

Angola

Zambia

Mozambique

Australia

Namibia

Zimbabwe

Madascar

Mauritus

Swaziland

INDIAN

South Africa

Lesotho

OCEAN

New Zealand

Saint
Lawrence
Island

Alaska

Kodiak
Island

Queen
Charlotte
Islands

Vancouver Island

Patrick Island

Ellesmere
Island

Axel
Heiberg
Island

Sverdrup Islands

Queen Elizabeth Islands

Banks
Island

Melville
Island

Devon Island

Prince
of
Wales
Island

Victoria Island

Baffin Island

Yukon
Territory

Northwest
Territories

Nunavut

British
Columbia

Alberta

Saskatchewan

Manitoba

C A N A D A

Newfoundland

Newfoundland

Ontario

Quebec

New
Brunswick

Prince
Edward
Island

Washington

Oregon

Montana

North Dakota

Minnesota

Nova Scotia

Idaho

Wyoming

South Dakota

Wisconsin

Michigan

Ottawa

Vermont

Maine

New Hampshire

Massachusetts

New York

Rhode Island
Connecticut

Nevada

U.S.A.

Iowa

Illinois

Indiana

Ohio

Pennsylvania

New Jersey

California

Utah

Colorado

Nebraska

Kansas

Missouri

West
Virginia

Virginia

Delaware
Maryland
Washington D. C.

Arizona

New Mexico

Oklahoma

Arkansas

Kentucky

Tennessee

North Carolina

South
Carolina

Texas

Mississippi

Alabama

Georgia

Hawaii

Louisiana

Florida

Puerto Rico

○ = state, province, or territory capital
◉ = country capital

United States Postal Abbreviations

Alabama	AL	Louisiana	LA	Ohio	OH
Alaska	AK	Maine	ME	Oklahoma	OK
Arizona	AZ	Maryland	MD	Oregon	OR
Arkansas	AR	Massachusetts	MA	Pennsylvania	PA
California	CA	Michigan	MI	Puerto Rico	PR
Colorado	CO	Minnesota	MN	Rhode Island	RI
Connecticut	CT	Mississippi	MS	South Carolina	SC
Delaware	DE	Missouri	MO	South Dakota	SD
District of Columbia	DC	Montana	MT	Tennessee	TN
Florida	FL	Nebraska	NE	Texas	TX
Georgia	GA	Nevada	NV	Utah	UT
Hawaii	HI	New Hampshire	NH	Vermont	VT
Idaho	ID	New Jersey	NJ	Virginia	VA
Illinois	IL	New Mexico	NM	Washington	WA
Indiana	IN	New York	NY	West Virginia	WV
Iowa	IA	North Carolina	NC	Wisconsin	WI
Kansas	KS	North Dakota	ND	Wyoming	WY
Kentucky	KY				

Canadian Postal Abbreviations

Alberta	AB	Newfoundland and Labrador	NL	Prince Edward Island	PE
British Columbia	BC	Northwest Territories	NT	Quebec	QC
Manitoba	MB	Nova Scotia	NS	Saskatchewan	SK
New Brunswick	NB	Nunavut	NU	Yukon	YT

United States Capitals

Alabama	Montgomery	Louisiana	Baton Rouge	Ohio	Columbus
Alaska	Juneau	Maine	Augusta	Oklahoma	Oklahoma City
Arizona	Phoenix	Maryland	Annapolis	Oregon	Salem
Arkansas	Little Rock	Massachusetts	Boston	Pennsylvania	Harrisburg
California	Sacramento	Michigan	Lansing	Rhode Island	Providence
Colorado	Denver	Minnesota	Saint Paul	South Carolina	Columbia
Connecticut	Hartford	Mississippi	Jackson	South Dakota	Pierre
Delaware	Dover	Missouri	Jefferson City	Tennessee	Nashville
Florida	Tallahassee	Montana	Helena	Texas	Austin
Georgia	Atlanta	Nebraska	Lincoln	Utah	Salt Lake City
Hawaii	Honolulu	Nevada	Carson City	Vermont	Montpelier
Idaho	Boise	New Hampshire	Concord	Virginia	Richmond
Illinois	Springfield	New Jersey	Trenton	Washington	Olympia
Indiana	Indianapolis	New Mexico	Santa Fe	West Virginia	Charleston
Iowa	Des Moines	New York	Albany	Wisconsin	Madison
Kansas	Topeka	North Carolina	Raleigh	Wyoming	Cheyenne
Kentucky	Frankfort	North Dakota	Bismarck		

Canadian Capitals

Alberta	Edmonton	Nova Scotia	Halifax
British Columbia	Victoria	Nunavut	Iqaluit
Manitoba	Winnipeg	Prince Edward Island	Charlottetown
New Brunswick	Fredericton	Quebec	Quebec City
Newfoundland and Labrador	St. John's	Saskatchewan	Regina
Northwest Territories	Yellowknife	Yukon	Whitehorse

Audioscript

Unit 1 Lesson 2

Practice, Exercise A page 4

A: What's your name?

B: Dimitri Levin.

A: How do you spell that?

B: D-I-M-I-T-R-I L-E-V-I-N.

A: What's your address?

B: 64 Elm Street, Teaneck, New Jersey 07666.

A: What's your phone number?

B: 201-555-4321.

A: What's your date of birth?

B: August 13, 1975.

A: What country are you from?

B: I'm from Russia.

Listen page 5

1.

A: What's your name?

B: Steven Johnson.

2.

A: What's your address?

B: 540 Alpine Street.

3.

A: What's your phone number?

B: 212-555-6543.

4.

A: What country are you from?

B: I'm from Chile.

5.

A: What's your date of birth?

B: August 30, 1984.

Unit 1 Lesson 3

Learn, Exercise A page 6

1. Monday to Thursday
2. from 7:00 to 9:30 P.M.
3. Monday, Wednesday, and Thursday
4. Tuesday and Thursday
5. on Monday

Unit 2 Lesson 1

Learn, Exercise A page 20

1. Oscar is her grandfather.
2. Teresa is her grandmother.
3. Carlos is her father.
4. Ana is her mother.
5. Diego is her uncle.
6. Clara is her aunt.
7. Luis is her brother.
8. Lydia is her sister-in-law.
9. Eduardo is her husband.
10. Maria is her cousin.
11. Vicente is her nephew.
12. Martha is her niece.
13. Gloria is her daughter.
14. Raul is her son-in-law.
15. Tomas is her son.
16. Silvia is her daughter-in-law.
17. Pedro is her grandson.
18. Sonia is her granddaughter.

Practice, Exercise A page 21

1. She's Alan's daughter.
2. He's Alan's son.
3. He's Alan's son-in-law.
4. He's Alan's grandson.
5. She's Alan's daughter-in-law.
6. They're Alan's granddaughters.

Unit 2 Lesson 3

Listen page 26

1. He's average height.
2. He's tall.
3. He has glasses.
4. He's a little heavy.
5. He has short, curly hair.
6. He has long, straight hair.
7. He has freckles.
8. He has a beard.
9. He's short.
10. He's a little bald.
11. He's average weight.
12. He has a mustache.

Unit 2 Lesson 4

Learn, Exercise B page 27

1. What an adorable baby!
2. What a pretty girl!
3. What a handsome young man!
4. What a kind man!
5. What a good-looking family!
6. What a thoughtful woman!
7. What a cute boy!
8. What a friendly man!
9. What a beautiful woman!

Practice, Exercise C page 28

1. What an adorable baby!
2. What a beautiful woman!
3. What a thoughtful man!
4. What a good-looking family!
5. What a pretty girl!
6. What a handsome young man!

Unit 3 Lesson 2

Learn, Exercise A page 37

A: Sam's Plumbing Company. May I help you?
B: May I speak with Sam Hall, please?
A: He's not in right now. May I take a message?
B: Yes, please tell him to call Mrs. Brannon.
A: How do you spell that?
B: B-R-A-N-N-O-N.
A: And what's the problem?
B: I have a problem with my kitchen sink.
A: What's your telephone number?
B: 213-555-6129.
A: Did you say 213-555-6129?
B: That's correct.
A: OK, I'll give him the message.
B: Thank you.

Practice, Exercise A page 38

A: Ace Plumbing Company. May I help you?
B: May I speak with Ben Johnson, please?
A: He's not in right now. May I take a message?
B: Yes, please tell him to call Pat James.
A: How do you spell that?
B: J-A-M-E-S.
A: And what's the problem?
B: I have a problem with my washing machine.
A: What's your telephone number?
B: 325-555-9834.

A: Did you say 325-555-9834?
B: That's correct.
A: OK, I'll give him the message.
B: Thank you.

Practice, Exercise B page 38

A: Good afternoon, Standard Computer Services. May I help you?
B: May I speak with Mrs. Anderson, please?
A: She's not in right now. May I take a message?
B: Yes, please tell her to call Bob Smith.
A: How do you spell that?
B: S-M-I-T-H.
A: And what's the problem?
B: My printer isn't working.
A: What's your phone number?
B: 401-555-3029.
A: Did you say 401-555-3029?
B: That's correct.
A: OK, I'll give her the message.
B: Thank you.

Unit 3 Lesson 3

Learn page 40

Thank you for calling Los Angeles Occupational Center. We are located at 3692 West Venice Boulevard in Los Angeles. For class and schedule information, press 1. For the Counseling and Testing Office, press 2. For the Computer Lab, press 3. For all other questions, or to leave a message, press zero.

Practice, Exercise A page 40

Thank you for calling Los Angeles Occupational Center. We are located at 3692 West Venice Boulevard in Los Angeles. For class and schedule information, press 1. For the Counseling and Testing Office, press 2. For the Computer Lab, press 3. For all other questions, or to leave a message, press zero.

Practice, Exercise B page 40

Thank you for calling TCC, your Telephone Communication Company. For English, press 1. For problems with your telephone service, press 2. For billing inquiries, press 3. For sales, press 4. To speak with a customer service representative, press zero.

Practice, Exercise C page 40

You have reached Millman's Department Store. For store hours, press 1. For store location, press 2. For directions to the store, press 3. For customer service and all other information, press 4.

Make It Yours, Exercise A page 41

You have reached the George Washington Library, located at 4100 South Washington Boulevard in Los Angeles. Our hours are from 10:00 A.M. to 8:00 P.M. Monday to Thursday, and from 10:00 A.M. to 6:00 P.M. on Friday and Saturday. We are closed on Sunday. To speak with a librarian, press 1.

Make It Yours, Exercise A page 41

You have reached Hudson Medical Associates. We are open Monday to Friday from 9:00 to 5:00. Our office is closed now. If this is a medical emergency, please press 1. For an appointment, please call back during regular business hours.

Unit 4 Lesson 2

Learn, Exercise B page 54

1. go to a concert
2. go to the park
3. go to a movie
4. go out for coffee
5. go to a party
6. go to a basketball game

Unit 4 Lesson 3

Learn, Exercise B page 56

1. The police station is on Pine Street.
2. The library is on the corner of Central Avenue and Pine Street.
3. The community center is between the library and the post office.
4. The parking lot is next to the mall.
5. The hospital is across from the mall and the parking lot.
6. The bus stop is in front of the hospital.

Learn, Exercise B page 57

A: Excuse me. How do I get to the mall?
B: The mall? Go east for one block. Go left on Park Avenue and go north for three blocks. It's on the left.
A: Thank you.

Listen page 59

1. The bank is on Central Avenue.
2. Go north on Maple Street for two blocks.
3. The hotel is on the left.
4. Go north on Western Boulevard for one block.

Unit 4 Lesson 5

Learn, Exercise A page 61

Express Mail
Priority Mail
First-Class Mail
Parcel Post

Unit 5 Lesson 1

Practice, Exercise B page 71

1. a box of cereal
2. a jar of jelly
3. a bottle of salad dressing
4. a container of milk
5. a package of muffins
6. a tub of cream cheese
7. a roll of toilet paper
8. a bag of potato chips
9. a can of soup

Unit 5 Lesson 3

Listen page 75

1. It has 700 milligrams of sodium.
2. A serving is a half cup.
3. It has 1.5 grams of total fat.
4. It has 35 calories from fat.
5. It has three servings per container.
6. It has three grams of protein.
7. It has 175 calories per serving.
8. It has ten grams of carbohydrates per serving.

Unit 5 Lesson 4

Learn page 77

Royal ham is $7.99 (seven ninety-nine) a pound.
Country Fresh ham is $8.99 (eight ninety-nine) a pound.
Best Farms eggs are $2.89 (two eighty-nine) a dozen.
Star organic eggs are $3.69 (three sixty-nine) a dozen.
Royal Swiss cheese is $6.25 (six twenty-five) a pound.
Country Fresh Swiss cheese is $7.50 (seven fifty) a pound.
Tasty tuna is $1.19 (one nineteen) for a seven-ounce can.
Food Mart tuna is $1.09 (one oh nine) for a seven-ounce can.

(continued)

Best Farms ice cream is $5.49 (five forty-nine) a half-gallon.
Star ice cream is $4.29 (four twenty-nine) a half-gallon.
U2 raisin bran is $3.50 (three fifty) for a 15-ounce box.
Food Mart raisin bran is $2.75 (two seventy-five) for
a 15-ounce box.

Unit 5 Lesson 5

Listen page 81

1.

A: What would you like?

B: I'd like a tuna salad sandwich.

A: Would you like tomato and lettuce?

B: Just lettuce.

What's the order?

2.

A: Are you ready to order?

B: Yes, I'd like a hamburger deluxe.

A: Would you like anything else?

B: A cup of soup, please.

What's the order?

3.

A: What would you like?

B: I'd like a turkey sandwich. Does it come with fries?

A: No, that's extra.

B: Oh, no fries then.

A: Would you like something to drink?

B: A cup of coffee, please.

What's the order?

Unit 6 Lesson 4

Listen page 97

1.

A: Can I help you?

B: Yes, do you have these shoes in size 8?

A: I think so. Let me check in the back.

What does the customer want?

2.

A: Can I help you?

B: Do you have these sneakers in white?

A: No, but we have them in black.

What's the problem?

3.

A: Can I help you?

B: Yes, I'm looking for these sandals in size 9.

A: Sorry, we're out of that size. We have them in size 8.

What size is he looking for?

4.

A: Can I help you?

B: Yes, do you have these boots in size 7?

A: Yes, we have them in stock in the back.

Where are the boots?

Unit 7 Lesson 1

Listen page 107

1. It's cold.

2. It's very hot.

3. It's hot.

4. It's warm.

5. It's very cold.

Unit 7 Lesson 3

Listen page 111

1. It's 180 miles from Springfield to Northville.

2. My home is 14 miles from the school.

3. It's 165 miles from my mother's house to my house.

4. My hometown is 66 miles from the airport.

5. It's 301 miles from Pleasanton to New York.

Unit 8 Lesson 1

Listen page 117

1.

A: Could you tell me about the apartment?

B: It has two bedrooms, a living room, a large kitchen, and a bathroom. The rent is $1,200. (twelve hundred dollars)

2.

A: Is there a dishwasher?

B: No, there isn't.

3.

A: Are the utilities included in the rent?

B: Heat and hot water are included.

4.

A: Is there parking?

B: Yes, and there's a bus stop on the corner.

Unit 8 Lesson 3

Learn, Exercise B page 120

1.

A: Can you help me?

B: What's the matter?

A: I can't get into my bedroom. The door is stuck!

2.

A: Uh-oh.

B: What's wrong?

A: Come in here and look. The plaster is falling from the ceiling.

3.

A: Oh, no!

B: What happened?

A: The sink in the kitchen is stopped up again.

4.

A: Uh-oh. This is a problem.

B: What is it?

A: You know we're having a party tomorrow, but the refrigerator isn't working.

5.

A: Could I use your phone?

B: Sure. What's the problem?

A: I can't get into my apartment. My lock is broken.

6.

A: Could you call a plumber, please?

B: Why? What's wrong?

A: The toilet is overflowing.

7.

A: Uh-oh. Do you have the number of the plumber?

B: Probably. Why?

A: The toilet isn't flushing!

8.

A: I think we need to call the landlord.

B: Why?

A: A pipe is leaking in the kitchen.

9.

A: Oh, no, not again.

B: What's wrong?

A: The faucet in the bathtub is dripping.

Listen page 121

1.

A: Hello. This is Mr. Harris in apartment 2B.

B: Yes, Mr. Harris. How can I help you?

A: The faucet in my kitchen sink is dripping. I can't shut it off.

B: I'll try to come by this week.

2.

A: Hello. This is Mrs. Montalvo in apartment 1D.

B: Yes, Mrs. Montalvo. How can I help you?

A: My toilet is overflowing.

B: I'll try to come by soon.

3.

A: Hello. This is Mrs. Patel in apartment 3C.

B: Yes, Mrs. Patel. How can I help you?

A: The window in my living room is stuck. I can't open it.

B: I'll try to come by this week.

Unit 9 Lesson 1

Learn, Exercise B page 126

1. head
2. neck
3. shoulder
4. back
5. elbow
6. wrist
7. hand
8. finger
9. thumb
10. buttocks
11. foot
12. throat
13. chest
14. breast
15. stomach
16. hip
17. thigh
18. knee
19. ankle
20. toe

Learn, Exercise B page 127

1. forehead
2. eyebrow
3. eyelashes
4. eye
5. ear
6. nose
7. cheek
8. lips
9. chin

Unit 9 Lesson 2

Learn, Exercise B page 129

1. I hurt my back.
2. I cut my foot.
3. I burned my hand.
4. I bruised my hip.
5. I sprained my ankle.
6. I broke my arm.

Unit 9 Lesson 3

Learn, Exercise B page 131

1. I have an infection.
2. I have a stiff neck.
3. I have a rash.
4. My eyes are itchy.
5. I have a stuffy nose.
6. I feel dizzy.
7. I have a sore throat.
8. I feel nauseous.

Unit 9 Lesson 7

Learn, Exercise B page 140

1. c. *Dosage* is how much medicine to take.
2. h. *Drowsiness* is sleepiness.
3. b. *Refill* is more medicine.
4. d. *As needed* is when you need it.
5. f. *Side effects* are bad reactions some people have to the medicine.
6. e. *Prescription number* is the number on your prescription label.
7. a. *Rx* is the abbreviation for *prescription*.

Listen page 140

1.
A: How much should I take?
B: Take one teaspoon.

2.
A: How often should I take this medicine?
B: Take it two times a day—morning and night.

3.
A: Should I take it with food?
B: Yes.

4.
A: What are its side effects?
B: This medicine may cause dizziness.

5.
A: Should I finish all the medicine?
B: Yes. Take it all.

6.
A: How many refills can I get?
B: None. There are no refills on this prescription.

Unit 10 Lesson 1

Learn, Exercise B page 148

1. b. Avoid contact with eyes.b.
2. a. Avoid contact with skin.
3. d. Avoid breathing in vapors.
4. e. Avoid mixing with other liquids.
5. c. Keep out of reach of children.
6. f. Keep away from heat.

Listen page 152

Conversation 1

A: My son poured drain cleaner on his hands.
B: Rinse his hands for fifteen to twenty minutes.

Conversation 2

A: My son drank some drain cleaner.
B: Don't induce vomiting. He should drink a glass of milk.

Conversation 3

A: My daughter sprayed some furniture polish in her eyes.
B: Flush her eyes with water for twenty minutes.

Unit 10 Lesson 3

Learn, Exercise B page 155

1. Freeze, don't move.
2. Step out of the car.
3. Put your hands behind your back.
4. Give me your license, registration, and insurance card.
5. Put up your hands.
6. Can I see your ID?
7. Put your hands on the car.

Unit 11 Lesson 1

Listen page 164

1. Jose works part-time.
2. The pay is $8.00 (eight dollars) an hour.
3. Experience is necessary.
4. You'll be working on weekends.
5. The benefits are excellent.
6. Experience is required.

Unit 12 Lesson 3

Learn, Exercise C page 178

On Tuesday, Brenda works from 7 to 3.
On Wednesday, she works from 7 to 3.
On Thursday, she works from 7 to 3.
On Friday, she works from 7 to 3.
On Saturday, she works from 7 to 3.
Brenda works the day shift.
Brenda works full-time, 40 hours a week.
She takes a one-hour lunch in the middle of her shift.

VALLEY HILL CLINIC   Medical History Form

Name _____ Date of Birth _____ Age _____

Home Address _____ Home Phone _____

Employer _____ Occupation _____

Work Address _____ Work Phone _____

ILLNESSES AND CONDITIONS
(Put an X by all that you have or have had in the past.)

( ) Asthma   ( ) HIV/AIDS   ( ) Migraines
( ) Cancer   ( ) Hay Fever   ( ) Mumps
( ) Chicken Pox   ( ) Heart Disease   ( ) Rheumatic Fever
( ) Ear Infection   ( ) Hypertension   ( ) Scarlet Fever
( ) Diabetes   ( ) Kidney Disease   ( ) Sinus Trouble
( ) Depression   ( ) Measles   ( ) Tuberculosis
( ) Epilepsy

ALLERGIES (Specify)

Animals _____ Medicine/Drugs _____

Food _____ Hay Fever/Pollen/Plants _____

Insect Stings _____ Other _____

	Yes	No
1. Have you ever been hospitalized, had a major operation, had a serious illness?	☐	☐
If yes, explain. _____		
2. Are you under medical treatment now?	☐	☐
If yes, explain. _____		
3. Are you pregnant?	☐	☐

ARE YOU TAKING PRESCRIPTION OR OVER-THE-COUNTER MEDICATION?

Medicine _____ Reason _____ Dosage _____

Medicine _____ Reason _____ Dosage _____

DO YOU HAVE HEALTH INSURANCE?

Name of Primary Insured _____

Social Security Number of Insured _____

Relationship to Patient _____

Insurance Carrier _____ Policy or Group Number _____

EMERGENCY CONTACT

Name _____ Phone Number _____ Relationship _____

_____ _____

Signature   Date

197

Sherry's Diner 🍴

Application for Employment

Sherry's Diner does not discriminate because of race, religion, color, sex, age, national origin, or marital status.

Personal Information:

Last Name: _____ First Name: _____ Middle Initial: _____

Home Address: _____ Apartment Number: _____ State: _____ Zip: _____

Home Phone: _____ E-mail: _____

Position applying for: _____ Date available to start work: _____

Are you over 18 years of age? _____ If not, date of birth: _____

Applying for: _____ Full Time _____ Part Time Available for overtime? _____

Have you ever been employed by Sherry's Diner? _____

Please list all times when you are available to work (from 5 A.M. until midnight)

Su. _____ M. _____ Tu. _____ W. _____ Th. _____ F. _____ Sa. _____

Education:

Last school attended (name of school): _____

Date last attended: _____

Employment History:

Employer Name: _____ Phone Number: _____

Street Address: _____ City: _____ State: _____

Employed from _____ to _____

Reason for leaving? _____ May we contact? _____

Employer Name: _____ Phone Number: _____

Street Address: _____ City: _____ State: _____

Employed from _____ to _____

Reason for leaving? _____ May we contact? _____

Employer Name: _____ Phone Number: _____

Street Address: _____ City: _____ State: _____

Employed from _____ to _____

Reason for leaving? _____ May we contact? _____

Qualifications and Experience:

Briefly describe your qualifications and experience below:

_____

_____

Signature: _____ Date: _____

Southeastern Industrial Warehouse

Accident Report

Name of Injured Employee: _____

Social Security Number: _____

Employee Job Title: _____

Length of Experience on Job: _____

Department: _____ Name of Supervisor: _____

Date of Accident: _____ Time of Accident: _____ Location of Accident: _____

Describe the accident and how it occurred.

_____

_____

_____

Witness(es): List name(s), department(s), and phone number(s).

_____

_____

_____

Did injured employee receive medical attention? _____

If yes, name and address of physician: _____

Has employee returned to work? _____

If no, expected date of return: _____

_____   _____

Signature   Date

Life Skills and Test Prep 2
Unit 1 Test Answer Sheet

① _____

Last Name   First Name   Middle

② _____

Teacher's Name

TEST

1 Ⓐ Ⓑ Ⓒ Ⓓ
2 Ⓐ Ⓑ Ⓒ Ⓓ
3 Ⓐ Ⓑ Ⓒ Ⓓ
4 Ⓐ Ⓑ Ⓒ Ⓓ
5 Ⓐ Ⓑ Ⓒ Ⓓ
6 Ⓐ Ⓑ Ⓒ Ⓓ
7 Ⓐ Ⓑ Ⓒ Ⓓ
8 Ⓐ Ⓑ Ⓒ Ⓓ
9 Ⓐ Ⓑ Ⓒ Ⓓ
10 Ⓐ Ⓑ Ⓒ Ⓓ
11 Ⓐ Ⓑ Ⓒ Ⓓ
12 Ⓐ Ⓑ Ⓒ Ⓓ
13 Ⓐ Ⓑ Ⓒ Ⓓ
14 Ⓐ Ⓑ Ⓒ Ⓓ
15 Ⓐ Ⓑ Ⓒ Ⓓ
16 Ⓐ Ⓑ Ⓒ Ⓓ
17 Ⓐ Ⓑ Ⓒ Ⓓ
18 Ⓐ Ⓑ Ⓒ Ⓓ
19 Ⓐ Ⓑ Ⓒ Ⓓ
20 Ⓐ Ⓑ Ⓒ Ⓓ

Directions for marking answers

- Use a No. 2 pencil. Do NOT use ink.
- Make dark marks and bubble in your answers completely.
- If you change an answer, erase your first mark completely.

Right
Ⓐ Ⓑ Ⓒ Ⓓ

Wrong
Ⓐ Ⓧ Ⓒ Ⓓ
Ⓐ Ⓑ Ⓒ Ⓓ

③ **STUDENT IDENTIFICATION**

Is this your Social Security number?
Yes ◯ No ◯

④ **TEST DATE**

MM	D	D	Y	Y
Jan ◯	0	0	200	0
Feb ◯	1	1	200	1
Mar ◯	2	2	200	2
Apr ◯	3	3	200	3
May ◯		4	200	4
Jun ◯		5	200	5
Jul ◯		6	200	6
Aug ◯		7	200	7
Sep ◯		8	200	8
Oct ◯		9	200	9
Nov ◯				
Dec ◯				

⑤ **CLASS NUMBER**

⑥ **RAW SCORE**

Life Skills and Test Prep 2
Unit 1 Test Answer Sheet

① _____

Last Name   First Name   Middle

② _____

Teacher's Name

TEST

1 Ⓐ Ⓑ Ⓒ Ⓓ

2 Ⓐ Ⓑ Ⓒ Ⓓ

3 Ⓐ Ⓑ Ⓒ Ⓓ

4 Ⓐ Ⓑ Ⓒ Ⓓ

5 Ⓐ Ⓑ Ⓒ Ⓓ

6 Ⓐ Ⓑ Ⓒ Ⓓ

7 Ⓐ Ⓑ Ⓒ Ⓓ

8 Ⓐ Ⓑ Ⓒ Ⓓ

9 Ⓐ Ⓑ Ⓒ Ⓓ

10 Ⓐ Ⓑ Ⓒ Ⓓ

11 Ⓐ Ⓑ Ⓒ Ⓓ

12 Ⓐ Ⓑ Ⓒ Ⓓ

13 Ⓐ Ⓑ Ⓒ Ⓓ

14 Ⓐ Ⓑ Ⓒ Ⓓ

15 Ⓐ Ⓑ Ⓒ Ⓓ

16 Ⓐ Ⓑ Ⓒ Ⓓ

17 Ⓐ Ⓑ Ⓒ Ⓓ

18 Ⓐ Ⓑ Ⓒ Ⓓ

19 Ⓐ Ⓑ Ⓒ Ⓓ

20 Ⓐ Ⓑ Ⓒ Ⓓ

Directions for marking answers

- Use a No. 2 pencil. Do NOT use ink.
- Make dark marks and bubble in your answers completely.
- If you change an answer, erase your first mark completely.

Right

Ⓐ ● Ⓒ Ⓓ

Wrong

Ⓐ ⊗ Ⓒ Ⓓ

Ⓐ Ⓑ Ⓒ Ⓓ

③ **STUDENT IDENTIFICATION**

Is this your Social Security number?
Yes ◯ No ◯

④ **TEST DATE**

MM	D	D	Y	Y
Jan	0	0	200	0
Feb	1	1	200	1
Mar	2	2	200	2
Apr	3	3	200	3
May		4	200	4
Jun		5	200	5
Jul		6	200	6
Aug		7	200	7
Sep		8	200	8
Oct		9	200	9
Nov				
Dec				

⑤ **CLASS NUMBER**

⑥ **RAW SCORE**

Life Skills and Test Prep 2
Unit 2 Test Answer Sheet

① _____

    Last Name   First Name   Middle

② _____

    Teacher's Name

TEST

1 (A) (B) (C) (D)
2 (A) (B) (C) (D)
3 (A) (B) (C) (D)
4 (A) (B) (C) (D)
5 (A) (B) (C) (D)
6 (A) (B) (C) (D)
7 (A) (B) (C) (D)
8 (A) (B) (C) (D)
9 (A) (B) (C) (D)
10 (A) (B) (C) (D)
11 (A) (B) (C) (D)
12 (A) (B) (C) (D)
13 (A) (B) (C) (D)
14 (A) (B) (C) (D)
15 (A) (B) (C) (D)
16 (A) (B) (C) (D)
17 (A) (B) (C) (D)
18 (A) (B) (C) (D)
19 (A) (B) (C) (D)
20 (A) (B) (C) (D)

Directions for marking answers

- Use a No. 2 pencil. Do NOT use ink.
- Make dark marks and bubble in your answers completely.
- If you change an answer, erase your first mark completely.

Right
(A) (B) (C) (D)

Wrong
(A) (X) (C) (D)
(A) (B) (C) (D)

③ **STUDENT IDENTIFICATION**

0	0	0	0	0	0	0	0	0
1	1	1	1	1	1	1	1	1
2	2	2	2	2	2	2	2	2
3	3	3	3	3	3	3	3	3
4	4	4	4	4	4	4	4	4
5	5	5	5	5	5	5	5	5
6	6	6	6	6	6	6	6	6
7	7	7	7	7	7	7	7	7
8	8	8	8	8	8	8	8	8
9	9	9	9	9	9	9	9	9

Is this your Social Security number?
Yes ⬭ No ⬭

④ **TEST DATE**

MM	D	D	Y	Y
Jan ⬭	0	0	200	0
Feb ⬭	1	1	200	1
Mar ⬭	2	2	200	2
Apr ⬭	3	3	200	3
May ⬭		4	200	4
Jun ⬭		5	200	5
Jul ⬭		6	200	6
Aug ⬭		7	200	7
Sep ⬭		8	200	8
Oct ⬭		9	200	9
Nov ⬭				
Dec ⬭				

⑤ **CLASS NUMBER**

0	0	0	0	0	0	0	0	0
1	1	1	1	1	1	1	1	1
2	2	2	2	2	2	2	2	2
3	3	3	3	3	3	3	3	3
4	4	4	4	4	4	4	4	4
5	5	5	5	5	5	5	5	5
6	6	6	6	6	6	6	6	6
7	7	7	7	7	7	7	7	7
8	8	8	8	8	8	8	8	8
9	9	9	9	9	9	9	9	9

⑥ **RAW SCORE**

0	0
1	1
2	2
3	3
4	4
5	5
6	6
7	7
8	8
9	9

Life Skills and Test Prep 2
Unit 2 Test Answer Sheet

① _____

    Last Name   First Name   Middle

② _____

    Teacher's Name

TEST

1 Ⓐ Ⓑ Ⓒ Ⓓ
2 Ⓐ Ⓑ Ⓒ Ⓓ
3 Ⓐ Ⓑ Ⓒ Ⓓ
4 Ⓐ Ⓑ Ⓒ Ⓓ
5 Ⓐ Ⓑ Ⓒ Ⓓ
6 Ⓐ Ⓑ Ⓒ Ⓓ
7 Ⓐ Ⓑ Ⓒ Ⓓ
8 Ⓐ Ⓑ Ⓒ Ⓓ
9 Ⓐ Ⓑ Ⓒ Ⓓ
10 Ⓐ Ⓑ Ⓒ Ⓓ
11 Ⓐ Ⓑ Ⓒ Ⓓ
12 Ⓐ Ⓑ Ⓒ Ⓓ
13 Ⓐ Ⓑ Ⓒ Ⓓ
14 Ⓐ Ⓑ Ⓒ Ⓓ
15 Ⓐ Ⓑ Ⓒ Ⓓ
16 Ⓐ Ⓑ Ⓒ Ⓓ
17 Ⓐ Ⓑ Ⓒ Ⓓ
18 Ⓐ Ⓑ Ⓒ Ⓓ
19 Ⓐ Ⓑ Ⓒ Ⓓ
20 Ⓐ Ⓑ Ⓒ Ⓓ

Directions for marking answers

- Use a No. 2 pencil. Do NOT use ink.
- Make dark marks and bubble in your answers completely.
- If you change an answer, erase your first mark completely.

Right
Ⓐ ● Ⓒ Ⓓ

Wrong
Ⓐ ⊗ Ⓒ Ⓓ
Ⓐ Ⓑ Ⓒ Ⓓ

③ STUDENT IDENTIFICATION

(grid of bubbles 0–9 across nine columns)

Is this your Social Security number?
Yes ◯ No ◯

④ TEST DATE

MM	D	D	Y	Y
Jan	0	0	200	0
Feb	1	1	200	1
Mar	2	2	200	2
Apr	3	3	200	3
May		4	200	4
Jun		5	200	5
Jul		6	200	6
Aug		7	200	7
Sep		8	200	8
Oct		9	200	9
Nov				
Dec				

⑤ CLASS NUMBER

(grid of bubbles 0–9 across eight columns)

⑥ RAW SCORE

(grid of bubbles 0–9 across two columns)

Life Skills and TEST Prep 2
Unit 3 Test Answer Sheet

① _____
  Last Name   First Name   Middle

② _____
  Teacher's Name

TEST

1 Ⓐ Ⓑ Ⓒ Ⓓ

2 Ⓐ Ⓑ Ⓒ Ⓓ

3 Ⓐ Ⓑ Ⓒ Ⓓ

4 Ⓐ Ⓑ Ⓒ Ⓓ

5 Ⓐ Ⓑ Ⓒ Ⓓ

6 Ⓐ Ⓑ Ⓒ Ⓓ

7 Ⓐ Ⓑ Ⓒ Ⓓ

8 Ⓐ Ⓑ Ⓒ Ⓓ

9 Ⓐ Ⓑ Ⓒ Ⓓ

10 Ⓐ Ⓑ Ⓒ Ⓓ

11 Ⓐ Ⓑ Ⓒ Ⓓ

12 Ⓐ Ⓑ Ⓒ Ⓓ

13 Ⓐ Ⓑ Ⓒ Ⓓ

14 Ⓐ Ⓑ Ⓒ Ⓓ

15 Ⓐ Ⓑ Ⓒ Ⓓ

16 Ⓐ Ⓑ Ⓒ Ⓓ

17 Ⓐ Ⓑ Ⓒ Ⓓ

18 Ⓐ Ⓑ Ⓒ Ⓓ

19 Ⓐ Ⓑ Ⓒ Ⓓ

20 Ⓐ Ⓑ Ⓒ Ⓓ

Directions for marking answers

- Use a No. 2 pencil. Do NOT use ink.
- Make dark marks and bubble in your answers completely.
- If you change an answer, erase your first mark completely.

Right
Ⓐ ⬤ Ⓒ Ⓓ

Wrong
Ⓐ ⓧ Ⓒ Ⓓ
Ⓐ Ⓑ Ⓒ Ⓓ

③ STUDENT IDENTIFICATION

0 0 0   0 0   0 0 0 0
1 1 1   1 1   1 1 1 1
2 2 2   2 2   2 2 2 2
3 3 3   3 3   3 3 3 3
4 4 4   4 4   4 4 4 4
5 5 5   5 5   5 5 5 5
6 6 6   6 6   6 6 6 6
7 7 7   7 7   7 7 7 7
8 8 8   8 8   8 8 8 8
9 9 9   9 9   9 9 9 9

Is this your Social Security number?
Yes ☐ No ☐

④ TEST DATE

MM	D	D	Y	Y
Jan	0	0	200	0
Feb	1	1	200	1
Mar	2	2	200	2
Apr	3	3	200	3
May		4	200	4
Jun		5	200	5
Jul		6	200	6
Aug		7	200	7
Sep		8	200	8
Oct		9	200	9
Nov				
Dec				

⑤ CLASS NUMBER

0 0 0 0 0 0 0 0 0
1 1 1 1 1 1 1 1 1
2 2 2 2 2 2 2 2 2
3 3 3 3 3 3 3 3 3
4 4 4 4 4 4 4 4 4
5 5 5 5 5 5 5 5 5
6 6 6 6 6 6 6 6 6
7 7 7 7 7 7 7 7 7
8 8 8 8 8 8 8 8 8
9 9 9 9 9 9 9 9 9

⑥ RAW SCORE

0 0
1 1
2 2
3 3
4 4
5 5
6 6
7 7
8 8
9 9

Life Skills and Test Prep 2
Unit 3 Test Answer Sheet

① _____
    Last Name   First Name   Middle

② _____
    Teacher's Name

TEST

1 Ⓐ Ⓑ Ⓒ Ⓓ
2 Ⓐ Ⓑ Ⓒ Ⓓ
3 Ⓐ Ⓑ Ⓒ Ⓓ
4 Ⓐ Ⓑ Ⓒ Ⓓ
5 Ⓐ Ⓑ Ⓒ Ⓓ
6 Ⓐ Ⓑ Ⓒ Ⓓ
7 Ⓐ Ⓑ Ⓒ Ⓓ
8 Ⓐ Ⓑ Ⓒ Ⓓ
9 Ⓐ Ⓑ Ⓒ Ⓓ
10 Ⓐ Ⓑ Ⓒ Ⓓ
11 Ⓐ Ⓑ Ⓒ Ⓓ
12 Ⓐ Ⓑ Ⓒ Ⓓ
13 Ⓐ Ⓑ Ⓒ Ⓓ
14 Ⓐ Ⓑ Ⓒ Ⓓ
15 Ⓐ Ⓑ Ⓒ Ⓓ
16 Ⓐ Ⓑ Ⓒ Ⓓ
17 Ⓐ Ⓑ Ⓒ Ⓓ
18 Ⓐ Ⓑ Ⓒ Ⓓ
19 Ⓐ Ⓑ Ⓒ Ⓓ
20 Ⓐ Ⓑ Ⓒ Ⓓ

Directions for marking answers

- Use a No. 2 pencil. Do NOT use ink.
- Make dark marks and bubble in your answers completely.
- If you change an answer, erase your first mark completely.

Right
Ⓐ ● Ⓒ Ⓓ

Wrong
Ⓐ ⊗ Ⓒ Ⓓ
Ⓐ Ⓑ Ⓒ Ⓓ

③ **STUDENT IDENTIFICATION**

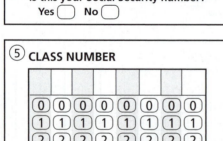

Is this your Social Security number?
Yes ⬭ No ⬭

④ **TEST DATE**

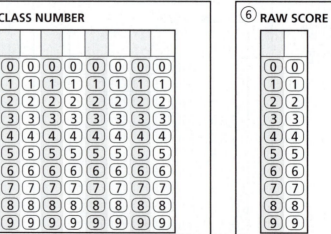

⑤ **CLASS NUMBER**

⑥ **RAW SCORE**

Life Skills and Test Prep 2
Unit 4 Test Answer Sheet

① _____
Last Name   First Name   Middle

② _____
Teacher's Name

TEST

1 Ⓐ Ⓑ Ⓒ Ⓓ
2 Ⓐ Ⓑ Ⓒ Ⓓ
3 Ⓐ Ⓑ Ⓒ Ⓓ
4 Ⓐ Ⓑ Ⓒ Ⓓ
5 Ⓐ Ⓑ Ⓒ Ⓓ
6 Ⓐ Ⓑ Ⓒ Ⓓ
7 Ⓐ Ⓑ Ⓒ Ⓓ
8 Ⓐ Ⓑ Ⓒ Ⓓ
9 Ⓐ Ⓑ Ⓒ Ⓓ
10 Ⓐ Ⓑ Ⓒ Ⓓ
11 Ⓐ Ⓑ Ⓒ Ⓓ
12 Ⓐ Ⓑ Ⓒ Ⓓ
13 Ⓐ Ⓑ Ⓒ Ⓓ
14 Ⓐ Ⓑ Ⓒ Ⓓ
15 Ⓐ Ⓑ Ⓒ Ⓓ
16 Ⓐ Ⓑ Ⓒ Ⓓ
17 Ⓐ Ⓑ Ⓒ Ⓓ
18 Ⓐ Ⓑ Ⓒ Ⓓ
19 Ⓐ Ⓑ Ⓒ Ⓓ
20 Ⓐ Ⓑ Ⓒ Ⓓ

Directions for marking answers

- Use a No. 2 pencil. Do NOT use ink.
- Make dark marks and bubble in your answers completely.
- If you change an answer, erase your first mark completely.

Right
Ⓐ ⬤ Ⓒ Ⓓ
Wrong
Ⓐ ⊗ Ⓒ Ⓓ
Ⓐ Ⓑ Ⓒ Ⓓ

③ **STUDENT IDENTIFICATION**

Is this your Social Security number?
Yes ⬚   No ⬚

④ **TEST DATE**

MM	D	D	Y	Y
Jan	0	0	200	0
Feb	1	1	200	1
Mar	2	2	200	2
Apr	3	3	200	3
May		4	200	4
Jun		5	200	5
Jul		6	200	6
Aug		7	200	7
Sep		8	200	8
Oct		9	200	9
Nov				
Dec				

⑤ **CLASS NUMBER**

⑥ **RAW SCORE**

Life Skills and Test Prep 2
Unit 4 Test Answer Sheet

① _____

   Last Name   First Name   Middle

② _____

   Teacher's Name

TEST

1 Ⓐ Ⓑ Ⓒ Ⓓ
2 Ⓐ Ⓑ Ⓒ Ⓓ
3 Ⓐ Ⓑ Ⓒ Ⓓ
4 Ⓐ Ⓑ Ⓒ Ⓓ
5 Ⓐ Ⓑ Ⓒ Ⓓ
6 Ⓐ Ⓑ Ⓒ Ⓓ
7 Ⓐ Ⓑ Ⓒ Ⓓ
8 Ⓐ Ⓑ Ⓒ Ⓓ
9 Ⓐ Ⓑ Ⓒ Ⓓ
10 Ⓐ Ⓑ Ⓒ Ⓓ
11 Ⓐ Ⓑ Ⓒ Ⓓ
12 Ⓐ Ⓑ Ⓒ Ⓓ
13 Ⓐ Ⓑ Ⓒ Ⓓ
14 Ⓐ Ⓑ Ⓒ Ⓓ
15 Ⓐ Ⓑ Ⓒ Ⓓ
16 Ⓐ Ⓑ Ⓒ Ⓓ
17 Ⓐ Ⓑ Ⓒ Ⓓ
18 Ⓐ Ⓑ Ⓒ Ⓓ
19 Ⓐ Ⓑ Ⓒ Ⓓ
20 Ⓐ Ⓑ Ⓒ Ⓓ

Directions for marking answers

- Use a No. 2 pencil. Do NOT use ink.
- Make dark marks and bubble in your answers completely.
- If you change an answer, erase your first mark completely.

Right
Ⓐ ⬤ Ⓒ Ⓓ

Wrong
Ⓐ ⊗ Ⓒ Ⓓ
Ⓐ Ⓑ Ⓒ Ⓓ

③ **STUDENT IDENTIFICATION**

Is this your Social Security number?
Yes ⬭   No ⬭

④ **TEST DATE**

| MM | D | D | Y | Y |

Jan, Feb, Mar, Apr, May, Jun, Jul, Aug, Sep, Oct, Nov, Dec

⑤ **CLASS NUMBER**

⑥ **RAW SCORE**

Life Skills and Test Prep 2
Unit 5 Test Answer Sheet

① _____

    Last Name   First Name   Middle

② _____

    Teacher's Name

TEST

1 (A) (B) (C) (D)
2 (A) (B) (C) (D)
3 (A) (B) (C) (D)
4 (A) (B) (C) (D)
5 (A) (B) (C) (D)
6 (A) (B) (C) (D)
7 (A) (B) (C) (D)
8 (A) (B) (C) (D)
9 (A) (B) (C) (D)
10 (A) (B) (C) (D)
11 (A) (B) (C) (D)
12 (A) (B) (C) (D)
13 (A) (B) (C) (D)
14 (A) (B) (C) (D)
15 (A) (B) (C) (D)
16 (A) (B) (C) (D)
17 (A) (B) (C) (D)
18 (A) (B) (C) (D)
19 (A) (B) (C) (D)
20 (A) (B) (C) (D)

Directions for marking answers

- Use a No. 2 pencil. Do NOT use ink.
- Make dark marks and bubble in your answers completely.
- If you change an answer, erase your first mark completely.

Right

(A) (●B) (C) (D)

Wrong

(A) (⊗) (C) (D)
(A) (Ⓑ) (C) (D)

③ STUDENT IDENTIFICATION

Is this your Social Security number?
Yes ☐ No ☐

④ TEST DATE

MM	D	D	Y	Y
Jan	0	0	200	0
Feb	1	1	200	1
Mar	2	2	200	2
Apr	3	3	200	3
May		4	200	4
Jun		5	200	5
Jul		6	200	6
Aug		7	200	7
Sep		8	200	8
Oct		9	200	9
Nov				
Dec				

⑤ CLASS NUMBER

⑥ RAW SCORE

Life Skills and Test Prep 2
Unit 5 Test Answer Sheet

① _____

      Last Name   First Name   Middle

② _____

      Teacher's Name

TEST

1 Ⓐ Ⓑ Ⓒ Ⓓ
2 Ⓐ Ⓑ Ⓒ Ⓓ
3 Ⓐ Ⓑ Ⓒ Ⓓ
4 Ⓐ Ⓑ Ⓒ Ⓓ
5 Ⓐ Ⓑ Ⓒ Ⓓ
6 Ⓐ Ⓑ Ⓒ Ⓓ
7 Ⓐ Ⓑ Ⓒ Ⓓ
8 Ⓐ Ⓑ Ⓒ Ⓓ
9 Ⓐ Ⓑ Ⓒ Ⓓ
10 Ⓐ Ⓑ Ⓒ Ⓓ
11 Ⓐ Ⓑ Ⓒ Ⓓ
12 Ⓐ Ⓑ Ⓒ Ⓓ
13 Ⓐ Ⓑ Ⓒ Ⓓ
14 Ⓐ Ⓑ Ⓒ Ⓓ
15 Ⓐ Ⓑ Ⓒ Ⓓ
16 Ⓐ Ⓑ Ⓒ Ⓓ
17 Ⓐ Ⓑ Ⓒ Ⓓ
18 Ⓐ Ⓑ Ⓒ Ⓓ
19 Ⓐ Ⓑ Ⓒ Ⓓ
20 Ⓐ Ⓑ Ⓒ Ⓓ

Directions for marking answers

- Use a No. 2 pencil. Do NOT use ink.
- Make dark marks and bubble in your answers completely.
- If you change an answer, erase your first mark completely.

Right
Ⓐ ⬤ Ⓒ Ⓓ
Wrong
Ⓐ ⊗ Ⓒ Ⓓ
Ⓐ Ⓑ Ⓒ Ⓓ

③ **STUDENT IDENTIFICATION**

Is this your Social Security number?
Yes ⬭   No ⬭

④ **TEST DATE**

MM	D	D	Y	Y
Jan	0	0	200	0
Feb	1	1	200	1
Mar	2	2	200	2
Apr	3	3	200	3
May		4	200	4
Jun		5	200	5
Jul		6	200	6
Aug		7	200	7
Sep		8	200	8
Oct		9	200	9
Nov				
Dec				

⑤ **CLASS NUMBER**

⑥ **RAW SCORE**

Life Skills and Test Prep 2
Unit 6 Test Answer Sheet

① _____

    Last Name   First Name   Middle

② _____

    Teacher's Name

TEST

1 Ⓐ Ⓑ Ⓒ Ⓓ
2 Ⓐ Ⓑ Ⓒ Ⓓ
3 Ⓐ Ⓑ Ⓒ Ⓓ
4 Ⓐ Ⓑ Ⓒ Ⓓ
5 Ⓐ Ⓑ Ⓒ Ⓓ
6 Ⓐ Ⓑ Ⓒ Ⓓ
7 Ⓐ Ⓑ Ⓒ Ⓓ
8 Ⓐ Ⓑ Ⓒ Ⓓ
9 Ⓐ Ⓑ Ⓒ Ⓓ
10 Ⓐ Ⓑ Ⓒ Ⓓ
11 Ⓐ Ⓑ Ⓒ Ⓓ
12 Ⓐ Ⓑ Ⓒ Ⓓ
13 Ⓐ Ⓑ Ⓒ Ⓓ
14 Ⓐ Ⓑ Ⓒ Ⓓ
15 Ⓐ Ⓑ Ⓒ Ⓓ
16 Ⓐ Ⓑ Ⓒ Ⓓ
17 Ⓐ Ⓑ Ⓒ Ⓓ
18 Ⓐ Ⓑ Ⓒ Ⓓ
19 Ⓐ Ⓑ Ⓒ Ⓓ
20 Ⓐ Ⓑ Ⓒ Ⓓ

Directions for marking answers

- Use a No. 2 pencil. Do NOT use ink.
- Make dark marks and bubble in your answers completely.
- If you change an answer, erase your first mark completely.

Right
Ⓐ ⬤Ⓑ Ⓒ Ⓓ

Wrong
Ⓐ ⊗ Ⓒ Ⓓ
Ⓐ Ⓑ Ⓒ Ⓓ

③ STUDENT IDENTIFICATION

0 0 0 0 0 0 0 0 0
1 1 1 1 1 1 1 1 1
2 2 2 2 2 2 2 2 2
3 3 3 3 3 3 3 3 3
4 4 4 4 4 4 4 4 4
5 5 5 5 5 5 5 5 5
6 6 6 6 6 6 6 6 6
7 7 7 7 7 7 7 7 7
8 8 8 8 8 8 8 8 8
9 9 9 9 9 9 9 9 9

Is this your Social Security number?
Yes ☐   No ☐

④ TEST DATE

MM	D	D	Y	Y
Jan	0	0	200	0
Feb	1	1	200	1
Mar	2	2	200	2
Apr	3	3	200	3
May		4	200	4
Jun		5	200	5
Jul		6	200	6
Aug		7	200	7
Sep		8	200	8
Oct		9	200	9
Nov				
Dec				

⑤ CLASS NUMBER

0 0 0 0 0 0 0 0
1 1 1 1 1 1 1 1
2 2 2 2 2 2 2 2
3 3 3 3 3 3 3 3
4 4 4 4 4 4 4 4
5 5 5 5 5 5 5 5
6 6 6 6 6 6 6 6
7 7 7 7 7 7 7 7
8 8 8 8 8 8 8 8
9 9 9 9 9 9 9 9

⑥ RAW SCORE

0 0
1 1
2 2
3 3
4 4
5 5
6 6
7 7
8 8
9 9

Life Skills and Test Prep 2
Unit 6 Test Answer Sheet

① _____
    Last Name   First Name   Middle

② _____
    Teacher's Name

TEST

1 Ⓐ Ⓑ Ⓒ Ⓓ
2 Ⓐ Ⓑ Ⓒ Ⓓ
3 Ⓐ Ⓑ Ⓒ Ⓓ
4 Ⓐ Ⓑ Ⓒ Ⓓ
5 Ⓐ Ⓑ Ⓒ Ⓓ
6 Ⓐ Ⓑ Ⓒ Ⓓ
7 Ⓐ Ⓑ Ⓒ Ⓓ
8 Ⓐ Ⓑ Ⓒ Ⓓ
9 Ⓐ Ⓑ Ⓒ Ⓓ
10 Ⓐ Ⓑ Ⓒ Ⓓ
11 Ⓐ Ⓑ Ⓒ Ⓓ
12 Ⓐ Ⓑ Ⓒ Ⓓ
13 Ⓐ Ⓑ Ⓒ Ⓓ
14 Ⓐ Ⓑ Ⓒ Ⓓ
15 Ⓐ Ⓑ Ⓒ Ⓓ
16 Ⓐ Ⓑ Ⓒ Ⓓ
17 Ⓐ Ⓑ Ⓒ Ⓓ
18 Ⓐ Ⓑ Ⓒ Ⓓ
19 Ⓐ Ⓑ Ⓒ Ⓓ
20 Ⓐ Ⓑ Ⓒ Ⓓ

Directions for marking answers

- Use a No. 2 pencil. Do NOT use ink.
- Make dark marks and bubble in your answers completely.
- If you change an answer, erase your first mark completely.

Right
Ⓐ ⬤B Ⓒ Ⓓ

Wrong
Ⓐ ⊗ Ⓒ Ⓓ
Ⓐ Ⓑ Ⓒ Ⓓ

③ STUDENT IDENTIFICATION

0	0	0	0	0	0	0	0	0
1	1	1	1	1	1	1	1	1
2	2	2	2	2	2	2	2	2
3	3	3	3	3	3	3	3	3
4	4	4	4	4	4	4	4	4
5	5	5	5	5	5	5	5	5
6	6	6	6	6	6	6	6	6
7	7	7	7	7	7	7	7	7
8	8	8	8	8	8	8	8	8
9	9	9	9	9	9	9	9	9

Is this your Social Security number?
Yes ⬭   No ⬭

④ TEST DATE

MM	D	D	Y	Y
Jan ⬭	0	0	200	0
Feb ⬭	1	1	200	1
Mar ⬭	2	2	200	2
Apr ⬭	3	3	200	3
May ⬭		4	200	4
Jun ⬭		5	200	5
Jul ⬭		6	200	6
Aug ⬭		7	200	7
Sep ⬭		8	200	8
Oct ⬭		9	200	9
Nov ⬭				
Dec ⬭				

⑤ CLASS NUMBER

0	0	0	0	0	0	0	0
1	1	1	1	1	1	1	1
2	2	2	2	2	2	2	2
3	3	3	3	3	3	3	3
4	4	4	4	4	4	4	4
5	5	5	5	5	5	5	5
6	6	6	6	6	6	6	6
7	7	7	7	7	7	7	7
8	8	8	8	8	8	8	8
9	9	9	9	9	9	9	9

⑥ RAW SCORE

0	0
1	1
2	2
3	3
4	4
5	5
6	6
7	7
8	8
9	9

214

Life Skills and Test Prep 2
Unit 7 Test Answer Sheet

① _____

Last Name   First Name   Middle

② _____

Teacher's Name

TEST

1 Ⓐ Ⓑ Ⓒ Ⓓ
2 Ⓐ Ⓑ Ⓒ Ⓓ
3 Ⓐ Ⓑ Ⓒ Ⓓ
4 Ⓐ Ⓑ Ⓒ Ⓓ
5 Ⓐ Ⓑ Ⓒ Ⓓ
6 Ⓐ Ⓑ Ⓒ Ⓓ
7 Ⓐ Ⓑ Ⓒ Ⓓ
8 Ⓐ Ⓑ Ⓒ Ⓓ
9 Ⓐ Ⓑ Ⓒ Ⓓ
10 Ⓐ Ⓑ Ⓒ Ⓓ
11 Ⓐ Ⓑ Ⓒ Ⓓ
12 Ⓐ Ⓑ Ⓒ Ⓓ
13 Ⓐ Ⓑ Ⓒ Ⓓ
14 Ⓐ Ⓑ Ⓒ Ⓓ
15 Ⓐ Ⓑ Ⓒ Ⓓ
16 Ⓐ Ⓑ Ⓒ Ⓓ
17 Ⓐ Ⓑ Ⓒ Ⓓ
18 Ⓐ Ⓑ Ⓒ Ⓓ
19 Ⓐ Ⓑ Ⓒ Ⓓ
20 Ⓐ Ⓑ Ⓒ Ⓓ

Directions for marking answers

- Use a No. 2 pencil. Do NOT use ink.
- Make dark marks and bubble in your answers completely.
- If you change an answer, erase your first mark completely.

Right
Ⓐ ⬤ Ⓒ Ⓓ

Wrong
Ⓐ ⓧ Ⓒ Ⓓ
Ⓐ Ⓑ Ⓒ Ⓓ

③ STUDENT IDENTIFICATION

(grid of bubbles 0–9)

Is this your Social Security number?
Yes ⬭   No ⬭

④ TEST DATE

MM	D	D	Y	Y
Jan	0	0	200	0
Feb	1	1	200	1
Mar	2	2	200	2
Apr	3	3	200	3
May		4	200	4
Jun		5	200	5
Jul		6	200	6
Aug		7	200	7
Sep		8	200	8
Oct		9	200	9
Nov				
Dec				

⑤ CLASS NUMBER

(grid of bubbles 0–9)

⑥ RAW SCORE

(grid of bubbles 0–9)

① _____

Last Name   First Name   Middle

② _____

Teacher's Name

TEST

1 Ⓐ Ⓑ Ⓒ Ⓓ
2 Ⓐ Ⓑ Ⓒ Ⓓ
3 Ⓐ Ⓑ Ⓒ Ⓓ
4 Ⓐ Ⓑ Ⓒ Ⓓ
5 Ⓐ Ⓑ Ⓒ Ⓓ
6 Ⓐ Ⓑ Ⓒ Ⓓ
7 Ⓐ Ⓑ Ⓒ Ⓓ
8 Ⓐ Ⓑ Ⓒ Ⓓ
9 Ⓐ Ⓑ Ⓒ Ⓓ
10 Ⓐ Ⓑ Ⓒ Ⓓ
11 Ⓐ Ⓑ Ⓒ Ⓓ
12 Ⓐ Ⓑ Ⓒ Ⓓ
13 Ⓐ Ⓑ Ⓒ Ⓓ
14 Ⓐ Ⓑ Ⓒ Ⓓ
15 Ⓐ Ⓑ Ⓒ Ⓓ
16 Ⓐ Ⓑ Ⓒ Ⓓ
17 Ⓐ Ⓑ Ⓒ Ⓓ
18 Ⓐ Ⓑ Ⓒ Ⓓ
19 Ⓐ Ⓑ Ⓒ Ⓓ
20 Ⓐ Ⓑ Ⓒ Ⓓ

Directions for marking answers

• Use a No. 2 pencil. Do NOT use ink.
• Make dark marks and bubble in your answers completely.
• If you change an answer, erase your first mark completely.

Right
Ⓐ ● Ⓒ Ⓓ

Wrong
Ⓐ ⊗ Ⓒ Ⓓ
Ⓐ Ⓑ Ⓒ Ⓓ

③ **STUDENT IDENTIFICATION**

0 0 0 0 0 0 0 0 0
1 1 1 1 1 1 1 1 1
2 2 2 2 2 2 2 2 2
3 3 3 3 3 3 3 3 3
4 4 4 4 4 4 4 4 4
5 5 5 5 5 5 5 5 5
6 6 6 6 6 6 6 6 6
7 7 7 7 7 7 7 7 7
8 8 8 8 8 8 8 8 8
9 9 9 9 9 9 9 9 9

Is this your Social Security number?
Yes ◯ No ◯

④ **TEST DATE**

MM	D	D	Y	Y
Jan ◯	0	0	200	0
Feb ◯	1	1	200	1
Mar ◯	2	2	200	2
Apr ◯	3	3	200	3
May ◯		4	200	4
Jun ◯		5	200	5
Jul ◯		6	200	6
Aug ◯		7	200	7
Sep ◯		8	200	8
Oct ◯		9	200	9
Nov ◯				
Dec ◯				

⑤ **CLASS NUMBER**

0 0 0 0 0 0 0 0
1 1 1 1 1 1 1 1
2 2 2 2 2 2 2 2
3 3 3 3 3 3 3 3
4 4 4 4 4 4 4 4
5 5 5 5 5 5 5 5
6 6 6 6 6 6 6 6
7 7 7 7 7 7 7 7
8 8 8 8 8 8 8 8
9 9 9 9 9 9 9 9

⑥ **RAW SCORE**

0 0
1 1
2 2
3 3
4 4
5 5
6 6
7 7
8 8
9 9

Life Skills and Test Prep 2
Unit 8 Test Answer Sheet

① _____

    Last Name   First Name   Middle

② _____

    Teacher's Name

TEST

1 Ⓐ Ⓑ Ⓒ Ⓓ
2 Ⓐ Ⓑ Ⓒ Ⓓ
3 Ⓐ Ⓑ Ⓒ Ⓓ
4 Ⓐ Ⓑ Ⓒ Ⓓ
5 Ⓐ Ⓑ Ⓒ Ⓓ
6 Ⓐ Ⓑ Ⓒ Ⓓ
7 Ⓐ Ⓑ Ⓒ Ⓓ
8 Ⓐ Ⓑ Ⓒ Ⓓ
9 Ⓐ Ⓑ Ⓒ Ⓓ
10 Ⓐ Ⓑ Ⓒ Ⓓ
11 Ⓐ Ⓑ Ⓒ Ⓓ
12 Ⓐ Ⓑ Ⓒ Ⓓ
13 Ⓐ Ⓑ Ⓒ Ⓓ
14 Ⓐ Ⓑ Ⓒ Ⓓ
15 Ⓐ Ⓑ Ⓒ Ⓓ
16 Ⓐ Ⓑ Ⓒ Ⓓ
17 Ⓐ Ⓑ Ⓒ Ⓓ
18 Ⓐ Ⓑ Ⓒ Ⓓ
19 Ⓐ Ⓑ Ⓒ Ⓓ
20 Ⓐ Ⓑ Ⓒ Ⓓ

Directions for marking answers

- Use a No. 2 pencil. Do NOT use ink.
- Make dark marks and bubble in your answers completely.
- If you change an answer, erase your first mark completely.

Right
Ⓐ ⬤ Ⓒ Ⓓ

Wrong
Ⓐ Ⓧ Ⓒ Ⓓ
Ⓐ Ⓑ Ⓒ Ⓓ

③ STUDENT IDENTIFICATION

Is this your Social Security number?
Yes ⬡ No ⬡

④ TEST DATE

MM	D	D	Y	Y
Jan	0	0	200	0
Feb	1	1	200	1
Mar	2	2	200	2
Apr	3	3	200	3
May		4	200	4
Jun		5	200	5
Jul		6	200	6
Aug		7	200	7
Sep		8	200	8
Oct		9	200	9
Nov				
Dec				

⑤ CLASS NUMBER

⑥ RAW SCORE

Life Skills and Test Prep 2
Unit 8 Test Answer Sheet

① _____

    Last Name   First Name   Middle

② _____

    Teacher's Name

TEST

1 Ⓐ Ⓑ Ⓒ Ⓓ
2 Ⓐ Ⓑ Ⓒ Ⓓ
3 Ⓐ Ⓑ Ⓒ Ⓓ
4 Ⓐ Ⓑ Ⓒ Ⓓ
5 Ⓐ Ⓑ Ⓒ Ⓓ
6 Ⓐ Ⓑ Ⓒ Ⓓ
7 Ⓐ Ⓑ Ⓒ Ⓓ
8 Ⓐ Ⓑ Ⓒ Ⓓ
9 Ⓐ Ⓑ Ⓒ Ⓓ
10 Ⓐ Ⓑ Ⓒ Ⓓ
11 Ⓐ Ⓑ Ⓒ Ⓓ
12 Ⓐ Ⓑ Ⓒ Ⓓ
13 Ⓐ Ⓑ Ⓒ Ⓓ
14 Ⓐ Ⓑ Ⓒ Ⓓ
15 Ⓐ Ⓑ Ⓒ Ⓓ
16 Ⓐ Ⓑ Ⓒ Ⓓ
17 Ⓐ Ⓑ Ⓒ Ⓓ
18 Ⓐ Ⓑ Ⓒ Ⓓ
19 Ⓐ Ⓑ Ⓒ Ⓓ
20 Ⓐ Ⓑ Ⓒ Ⓓ

Directions for marking answers

- Use a No. 2 pencil. Do NOT use ink.
- Make dark marks and bubble in your answers completely.
- If you change an answer, erase your first mark completely.

Right
Ⓐ ● Ⓒ Ⓓ

Wrong
Ⓐ ⊗ Ⓒ Ⓓ
Ⓐ Ⓑ Ⓒ Ⓓ

③ STUDENT IDENTIFICATION

0 0 0	0 0	0 0 0 0
1 1 1	1 1	1 1 1 1
2 2 2	2 2	2 2 2 2
3 3 3	3 3	3 3 3 3
4 4 4	4 4	4 4 4 4
5 5 5	5 5	5 5 5 5
6 6 6	6 6	6 6 6 6
7 7 7	7 7	7 7 7 7
8 8 8	8 8	8 8 8 8
9 9 9	9 9	9 9 9 9

Is this your Social Security number?
Yes ☐ No ☐

④ TEST DATE

MM	D	D	Y	Y
Jan ☐	0	0	200	0
Feb ☐	1	1	200	1
Mar ☐	2	2	200	2
Apr ☐	3	3	200	3
May ☐		4	200	4
Jun ☐		5	200	5
Jul ☐		6	200	6
Aug ☐		7	200	7
Sep ☐		8	200	8
Oct ☐		9	200	9
Nov ☐				
Dec ☐				

⑤ CLASS NUMBER

| 0 0 0 0 0 0 0 0 |
| 1 1 1 1 1 1 1 1 |
| 2 2 2 2 2 2 2 2 |
| 3 3 3 3 3 3 3 3 |
| 4 4 4 4 4 4 4 4 |
| 5 5 5 5 5 5 5 5 |
| 6 6 6 6 6 6 6 6 |
| 7 7 7 7 7 7 7 7 |
| 8 8 8 8 8 8 8 8 |
| 9 9 9 9 9 9 9 9 |

⑥ RAW SCORE

| 0 0 |
| 1 1 |
| 2 2 |
| 3 3 |
| 4 4 |
| 5 5 |
| 6 6 |
| 7 7 |
| 8 8 |
| 9 9 |

Life Skills and Test Prep 2
Unit 9 Test Answer Sheet

① _____

    Last Name   First Name   Middle

② _____

    Teacher's Name

TEST

1 Ⓐ Ⓑ Ⓒ Ⓓ
2 Ⓐ Ⓑ Ⓒ Ⓓ
3 Ⓐ Ⓑ Ⓒ Ⓓ
4 Ⓐ Ⓑ Ⓒ Ⓓ
5 Ⓐ Ⓑ Ⓒ Ⓓ
6 Ⓐ Ⓑ Ⓒ Ⓓ
7 Ⓐ Ⓑ Ⓒ Ⓓ
8 Ⓐ Ⓑ Ⓒ Ⓓ
9 Ⓐ Ⓑ Ⓒ Ⓓ
10 Ⓐ Ⓑ Ⓒ Ⓓ
11 Ⓐ Ⓑ Ⓒ Ⓓ
12 Ⓐ Ⓑ Ⓒ Ⓓ
13 Ⓐ Ⓑ Ⓒ Ⓓ
14 Ⓐ Ⓑ Ⓒ Ⓓ
15 Ⓐ Ⓑ Ⓒ Ⓓ
16 Ⓐ Ⓑ Ⓒ Ⓓ
17 Ⓐ Ⓑ Ⓒ Ⓓ
18 Ⓐ Ⓑ Ⓒ Ⓓ
19 Ⓐ Ⓑ Ⓒ Ⓓ
20 Ⓐ Ⓑ Ⓒ Ⓓ

Directions for marking answers

- Use a No. 2 pencil. Do NOT use ink.
- Make dark marks and bubble in your answers completely.
- If you change an answer, erase your first mark completely.

Right
Ⓐ **Ⓑ** Ⓒ Ⓓ

Wrong
Ⓐ ⊠ Ⓒ Ⓓ
Ⓐ ⓑ Ⓒ Ⓓ

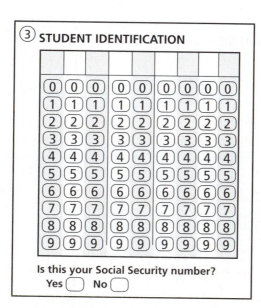

③ STUDENT IDENTIFICATION

Is this your Social Security number?
Yes ☐   No ☐

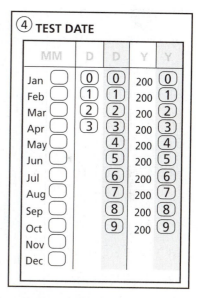

④ TEST DATE

⑤ CLASS NUMBER

⑥ RAW SCORE

(1) _____

Last Name   First Name   Middle

(2) _____

Teacher's Name

TEST

1 Ⓐ Ⓑ Ⓒ Ⓓ
2 Ⓐ Ⓑ Ⓒ Ⓓ
3 Ⓐ Ⓑ Ⓒ Ⓓ
4 Ⓐ Ⓑ Ⓒ Ⓓ
5 Ⓐ Ⓑ Ⓒ Ⓓ
6 Ⓐ Ⓑ Ⓒ Ⓓ
7 Ⓐ Ⓑ Ⓒ Ⓓ
8 Ⓐ Ⓑ Ⓒ Ⓓ
9 Ⓐ Ⓑ Ⓒ Ⓓ
10 Ⓐ Ⓑ Ⓒ Ⓓ
11 Ⓐ Ⓑ Ⓒ Ⓓ
12 Ⓐ Ⓑ Ⓒ Ⓓ
13 Ⓐ Ⓑ Ⓒ Ⓓ
14 Ⓐ Ⓑ Ⓒ Ⓓ
15 Ⓐ Ⓑ Ⓒ Ⓓ
16 Ⓐ Ⓑ Ⓒ Ⓓ
17 Ⓐ Ⓑ Ⓒ Ⓓ
18 Ⓐ Ⓑ Ⓒ Ⓓ
19 Ⓐ Ⓑ Ⓒ Ⓓ
20 Ⓐ Ⓑ Ⓒ Ⓓ

Directions for marking answers

- Use a No. 2 pencil. Do NOT use ink.
- Make dark marks and bubble in your answers completely.
- If you change an answer, erase your first mark completely.

Right
Ⓐ ● Ⓒ Ⓓ

Wrong
Ⓐ ⊗ Ⓒ Ⓓ
Ⓐ Ⓑ Ⓒ Ⓓ

(3) **STUDENT IDENTIFICATION**

0 0 0 | 0 0 | 0 0 0 0
1 1 1 | 1 1 | 1 1 1 1
2 2 2 | 2 2 | 2 2 2 2
3 3 3 | 3 3 | 3 3 3 3
4 4 4 | 4 4 | 4 4 4 4
5 5 5 | 5 5 | 5 5 5 5
6 6 6 | 6 6 | 6 6 6 6
7 7 7 | 7 7 | 7 7 7 7
8 8 8 | 8 8 | 8 8 8 8
9 9 9 | 9 9 | 9 9 9 9

Is this your Social Security number?
Yes ⬭   No ⬭

(4) **TEST DATE**

MM	D	D	Y	Y
Jan	0	0	200	0
Feb	1	1	200	1
Mar	2	2	200	2
Apr	3	3	200	3
May		4	200	4
Jun		5	200	5
Jul		6	200	6
Aug		7	200	7
Sep		8	200	8
Oct		9	200	9
Nov				
Dec				

(5) **CLASS NUMBER**

0 0 0 0 0 0 0 0
1 1 1 1 1 1 1 1
2 2 2 2 2 2 2 2
3 3 3 3 3 3 3 3
4 4 4 4 4 4 4 4
5 5 5 5 5 5 5 5
6 6 6 6 6 6 6 6
7 7 7 7 7 7 7 7
8 8 8 8 8 8 8 8
9 9 9 9 9 9 9 9

(6) **RAW SCORE**

0 0
1 1
2 2
3 3
4 4
5 5
6 6
7 7
8 8
9 9

Life Skills and Test Prep 2
Unit 10 Test Answer Sheet

① _____

Last Name   First Name   Middle

② _____

Teacher's Name

TEST

1 Ⓐ Ⓑ Ⓒ Ⓓ
2 Ⓐ Ⓑ Ⓒ Ⓓ
3 Ⓐ Ⓑ Ⓒ Ⓓ
4 Ⓐ Ⓑ Ⓒ Ⓓ
5 Ⓐ Ⓑ Ⓒ Ⓓ
6 Ⓐ Ⓑ Ⓒ Ⓓ
7 Ⓐ Ⓑ Ⓒ Ⓓ
8 Ⓐ Ⓑ Ⓒ Ⓓ
9 Ⓐ Ⓑ Ⓒ Ⓓ
10 Ⓐ Ⓑ Ⓒ Ⓓ
11 Ⓐ Ⓑ Ⓒ Ⓓ
12 Ⓐ Ⓑ Ⓒ Ⓓ
13 Ⓐ Ⓑ Ⓒ Ⓓ
14 Ⓐ Ⓑ Ⓒ Ⓓ
15 Ⓐ Ⓑ Ⓒ Ⓓ
16 Ⓐ Ⓑ Ⓒ Ⓓ
17 Ⓐ Ⓑ Ⓒ Ⓓ
18 Ⓐ Ⓑ Ⓒ Ⓓ
19 Ⓐ Ⓑ Ⓒ Ⓓ
20 Ⓐ Ⓑ Ⓒ Ⓓ

Directions for marking answers

- Use a No. 2 pencil. Do NOT use ink.
- Make dark marks and bubble in your answers completely.
- If you change an answer, erase your first mark completely.

Right
Ⓐ Ⓑ Ⓒ Ⓓ

Wrong
Ⓐ Ⓧ Ⓒ Ⓓ
Ⓐ Ⓑ Ⓒ Ⓓ

③ **STUDENT IDENTIFICATION**

Is this your Social Security number?
Yes ◯ No ◯

④ **TEST DATE**

MM	D	D	Y	Y
Jan	0	0	200	0
Feb	1	1	200	1
Mar	2	2	200	2
Apr	3	3	200	3
May		4	200	4
Jun		5	200	5
Jul		6	200	6
Aug		7	200	7
Sep		8	200	8
Oct		9	200	9
Nov				
Dec				

⑤ **CLASS NUMBER**

⑥ **RAW SCORE**

Life Skills and Test Prep 2
Unit 10 Test Answer Sheet

1 _____
   Last Name   First Name   Middle

2 _____
   Teacher's Name

TEST

1 Ⓐ Ⓑ Ⓒ Ⓓ
2 Ⓐ Ⓑ Ⓒ Ⓓ
3 Ⓐ Ⓑ Ⓒ Ⓓ
4 Ⓐ Ⓑ Ⓒ Ⓓ
5 Ⓐ Ⓑ Ⓒ Ⓓ
6 Ⓐ Ⓑ Ⓒ Ⓓ
7 Ⓐ Ⓑ Ⓒ Ⓓ
8 Ⓐ Ⓑ Ⓒ Ⓓ
9 Ⓐ Ⓑ Ⓒ Ⓓ
10 Ⓐ Ⓑ Ⓒ Ⓓ
11 Ⓐ Ⓑ Ⓒ Ⓓ
12 Ⓐ Ⓑ Ⓒ Ⓓ
13 Ⓐ Ⓑ Ⓒ Ⓓ
14 Ⓐ Ⓑ Ⓒ Ⓓ
15 Ⓐ Ⓑ Ⓒ Ⓓ
16 Ⓐ Ⓑ Ⓒ Ⓓ
17 Ⓐ Ⓑ Ⓒ Ⓓ
18 Ⓐ Ⓑ Ⓒ Ⓓ
19 Ⓐ Ⓑ Ⓒ Ⓓ
20 Ⓐ Ⓑ Ⓒ Ⓓ

Directions for marking answers

- Use a No. 2 pencil. Do NOT use ink.
- Make dark marks and bubble in your answers completely.
- If you change an answer, erase your first mark completely.

Right
Ⓐ ⬤ Ⓒ Ⓓ

Wrong
Ⓐ ⊗ Ⓒ Ⓓ
Ⓐ Ⓑ⃝ Ⓒ Ⓓ

③ **STUDENT IDENTIFICATION**

0 0 0	0 0 0	0 0 0
1 1 1	1 1 1	1 1 1
2 2 2	2 2 2	2 2 2
3 3 3	3 3 3	3 3 3
4 4 4	4 4 4	4 4 4
5 5 5	5 5 5	5 5 5
6 6 6	6 6 6	6 6 6
7 7 7	7 7 7	7 7 7
8 8 8	8 8 8	8 8 8
9 9 9	9 9 9	9 9 9

Is this your Social Security number?
Yes ◯   No ◯

④ **TEST DATE**

MM	D	D	Y	Y
Jan		0	0	200	0
Feb		1	1	200	1
Mar		2	2	200	2
Apr		3	3	200	3
May			4	200	4
Jun			5	200	5
Jul			6	200	6
Aug			7	200	7
Sep			8	200	8
Oct			9	200	9
Nov					
Dec					

⑤ **CLASS NUMBER**

| 0 0 0 0 0 0 0 0 |
| 1 1 1 1 1 1 1 1 |
| 2 2 2 2 2 2 2 2 |
| 3 3 3 3 3 3 3 3 |
| 4 4 4 4 4 4 4 4 |
| 5 5 5 5 5 5 5 5 |
| 6 6 6 6 6 6 6 6 |
| 7 7 7 7 7 7 7 7 |
| 8 8 8 8 8 8 8 8 |
| 9 9 9 9 9 9 9 9 |

⑥ **RAW SCORE**

| 0 0 |
| 1 1 |
| 2 2 |
| 3 3 |
| 4 4 |
| 5 5 |
| 6 6 |
| 7 7 |
| 8 8 |
| 9 9 |

① _____

    Last Name   First Name   Middle

② _____

    Teacher's Name

TEST

1 Ⓐ Ⓑ Ⓒ Ⓓ
2 Ⓐ Ⓑ Ⓒ Ⓓ
3 Ⓐ Ⓑ Ⓒ Ⓓ
4 Ⓐ Ⓑ Ⓒ Ⓓ
5 Ⓐ Ⓑ Ⓒ Ⓓ
6 Ⓐ Ⓑ Ⓒ Ⓓ
7 Ⓐ Ⓑ Ⓒ Ⓓ
8 Ⓐ Ⓑ Ⓒ Ⓓ
9 Ⓐ Ⓑ Ⓒ Ⓓ
10 Ⓐ Ⓑ Ⓒ Ⓓ
11 Ⓐ Ⓑ Ⓒ Ⓓ
12 Ⓐ Ⓑ Ⓒ Ⓓ
13 Ⓐ Ⓑ Ⓒ Ⓓ
14 Ⓐ Ⓑ Ⓒ Ⓓ
15 Ⓐ Ⓑ Ⓒ Ⓓ
16 Ⓐ Ⓑ Ⓒ Ⓓ
17 Ⓐ Ⓑ Ⓒ Ⓓ
18 Ⓐ Ⓑ Ⓒ Ⓓ
19 Ⓐ Ⓑ Ⓒ Ⓓ
20 Ⓐ Ⓑ Ⓒ Ⓓ

Directions for marking answers

- Use a No. 2 pencil. Do NOT use ink.
- Make dark marks and bubble in your answers completely.
- If you change an answer, erase your first mark completely.

Right
Ⓐ ⬤Ⓑ Ⓒ Ⓓ

Wrong
Ⓐ ⊗ Ⓒ Ⓓ
Ⓐ Ⓑ Ⓒ Ⓓ

③ **STUDENT IDENTIFICATION**

0 0 0   0 0   0 0   0 0
1 1 1   1 1   1 1   1 1
2 2 2   2 2   2 2   2 2
3 3 3   3 3   3 3   3 3
4 4 4   4 4   4 4   4 4
5 5 5   5 5   5 5   5 5
6 6 6   6 6   6 6   6 6
7 7 7   7 7   7 7   7 7
8 8 8   8 8   8 8   8 8
9 9 9   9 9   9 9   9 9

Is this your Social Security number?
Yes ⬭   No ⬭

④ **TEST DATE**

MM	D	D	Y	Y
Jan ⬭	0	0	200	0
Feb ⬭	1	1	200	1
Mar ⬭	2	2	200	2
Apr ⬭	3	3	200	3
May ⬭		4	200	4
Jun ⬭		5	200	5
Jul ⬭		6	200	6
Aug ⬭		7	200	7
Sep ⬭		8	200	8
Oct ⬭		9	200	9
Nov ⬭				
Dec ⬭				

⑤ **CLASS NUMBER**

0 0 0 0 0 0 0 0
1 1 1 1 1 1 1 1
2 2 2 2 2 2 2 2
3 3 3 3 3 3 3 3
4 4 4 4 4 4 4 4
5 5 5 5 5 5 5 5
6 6 6 6 6 6 6 6
7 7 7 7 7 7 7 7
8 8 8 8 8 8 8 8
9 9 9 9 9 9 9 9

⑥ **RAW SCORE**

0 0
1 1
2 2
3 3
4 4
5 5
6 6
7 7
8 8
9 9

① _____
　Last Name　　　　　　　First Name　　　　　Middle

② _____
　Teacher's Name

TEST

1 Ⓐ Ⓑ Ⓒ Ⓓ
2 Ⓐ Ⓑ Ⓒ Ⓓ
3 Ⓐ Ⓑ Ⓒ Ⓓ
4 Ⓐ Ⓑ Ⓒ Ⓓ
5 Ⓐ Ⓑ Ⓒ Ⓓ
6 Ⓐ Ⓑ Ⓒ Ⓓ
7 Ⓐ Ⓑ Ⓒ Ⓓ
8 Ⓐ Ⓑ Ⓒ Ⓓ
9 Ⓐ Ⓑ Ⓒ Ⓓ
10 Ⓐ Ⓑ Ⓒ Ⓓ
11 Ⓐ Ⓑ Ⓒ Ⓓ
12 Ⓐ Ⓑ Ⓒ Ⓓ
13 Ⓐ Ⓑ Ⓒ Ⓓ
14 Ⓐ Ⓑ Ⓒ Ⓓ
15 Ⓐ Ⓑ Ⓒ Ⓓ
16 Ⓐ Ⓑ Ⓒ Ⓓ
17 Ⓐ Ⓑ Ⓒ Ⓓ
18 Ⓐ Ⓑ Ⓒ Ⓓ
19 Ⓐ Ⓑ Ⓒ Ⓓ
20 Ⓐ Ⓑ Ⓒ Ⓓ

Directions for marking answers

- Use a No. 2 pencil. Do NOT use ink.
- Make dark marks and bubble in your answers completely.
- If you change an answer, erase your first mark completely.

Right
Ⓐ ⬤ Ⓒ Ⓓ
Wrong
Ⓐ ⓧ Ⓒ Ⓓ
Ⓐ Ⓑ Ⓒ Ⓓ

③ **STUDENT IDENTIFICATION**

0	0	0	0	0	0	0	0	0
1	1	1	1	1	1	1	1	1
2	2	2	2	2	2	2	2	2
3	3	3	3	3	3	3	3	3
4	4	4	4	4	4	4	4	4
5	5	5	5	5	5	5	5	5
6	6	6	6	6	6	6	6	6
7	7	7	7	7	7	7	7	7
8	8	8	8	8	8	8	8	8
9	9	9	9	9	9	9	9	9

Is this your Social Security number?
Yes ⬜　No ⬜

④ **TEST DATE**

MM	D	D	Y	Y
Jan	0	0	200	0
Feb	1	1	200	1
Mar	2	2	200	2
Apr	3	3	200	3
May		4	200	4
Jun		5	200	5
Jul		6	200	6
Aug		7	200	7
Sep		8	200	8
Oct		9	200	9
Nov				
Dec				

⑤ **CLASS NUMBER**

0	0	0	0	0	0	0	0
1	1	1	1	1	1	1	1
2	2	2	2	2	2	2	2
3	3	3	3	3	3	3	3
4	4	4	4	4	4	4	4
5	5	5	5	5	5	5	5
6	6	6	6	6	6	6	6
7	7	7	7	7	7	7	7
8	8	8	8	8	8	8	8
9	9	9	9	9	9	9	9

⑥ **RAW SCORE**

0	0
1	1
2	2
3	3
4	4
5	5
6	6
7	7
8	8
9	9

Life Skills and Test Prep 2
Unit 12 Test Answer Sheet

① _____

   Last Name   First Name   Middle

② _____

   Teacher's Name

TEST

1 Ⓐ Ⓑ Ⓒ Ⓓ
2 Ⓐ Ⓑ Ⓒ Ⓓ
3 Ⓐ Ⓑ Ⓒ Ⓓ
4 Ⓐ Ⓑ Ⓒ Ⓓ
5 Ⓐ Ⓑ Ⓒ Ⓓ
6 Ⓐ Ⓑ Ⓒ Ⓓ
7 Ⓐ Ⓑ Ⓒ Ⓓ
8 Ⓐ Ⓑ Ⓒ Ⓓ
9 Ⓐ Ⓑ Ⓒ Ⓓ
10 Ⓐ Ⓑ Ⓒ Ⓓ
11 Ⓐ Ⓑ Ⓒ Ⓓ
12 Ⓐ Ⓑ Ⓒ Ⓓ
13 Ⓐ Ⓑ Ⓒ Ⓓ
14 Ⓐ Ⓑ Ⓒ Ⓓ
15 Ⓐ Ⓑ Ⓒ Ⓓ
16 Ⓐ Ⓑ Ⓒ Ⓓ
17 Ⓐ Ⓑ Ⓒ Ⓓ
18 Ⓐ Ⓑ Ⓒ Ⓓ
19 Ⓐ Ⓑ Ⓒ Ⓓ
20 Ⓐ Ⓑ Ⓒ Ⓓ

Directions for marking answers

- Use a No. 2 pencil. Do NOT use ink.
- Make dark marks and bubble in your answers completely.
- If you change an answer, erase your first mark completely.

Right
Ⓐ ⬤Ⓑ Ⓒ Ⓓ

Wrong
Ⓐ Ⓧ Ⓒ Ⓓ
Ⓐ Ⓑ Ⓒ Ⓓ

③ **STUDENT IDENTIFICATION**

(bubble grid, digits 0–9 in nine columns)

Is this your Social Security number?
Yes ◯   No ◯

④ **TEST DATE**

MM	D	D	Y	Y
Jan ◯	⓪	⓪	200	⓪
Feb ◯	①	①	200	①
Mar ◯	②	②	200	②
Apr ◯	③	③	200	③
May ◯		④	200	④
Jun ◯		⑤	200	⑤
Jul ◯		⑥	200	⑥
Aug ◯		⑦	200	⑦
Sep ◯		⑧	200	⑧
Oct ◯		⑨	200	⑨
Nov ◯				
Dec ◯				

⑤ **CLASS NUMBER**

(bubble grid, digits 0–9 in nine columns)

⑥ **RAW SCORE**

(bubble grid, digits 0–9 in two columns)

Life Skills and Test Prep 2
Unit 12 Test Answer Sheet

① _____

    Last Name   First Name   Middle

② _____

    Teacher's Name

TEST

1 Ⓐ Ⓑ Ⓒ Ⓓ
2 Ⓐ Ⓑ Ⓒ Ⓓ
3 Ⓐ Ⓑ Ⓒ Ⓓ
4 Ⓐ Ⓑ Ⓒ Ⓓ
5 Ⓐ Ⓑ Ⓒ Ⓓ
6 Ⓐ Ⓑ Ⓒ Ⓓ
7 Ⓐ Ⓑ Ⓒ Ⓓ
8 Ⓐ Ⓑ Ⓒ Ⓓ
9 Ⓐ Ⓑ Ⓒ Ⓓ
10 Ⓐ Ⓑ Ⓒ Ⓓ
11 Ⓐ Ⓑ Ⓒ Ⓓ
12 Ⓐ Ⓑ Ⓒ Ⓓ
13 Ⓐ Ⓑ Ⓒ Ⓓ
14 Ⓐ Ⓑ Ⓒ Ⓓ
15 Ⓐ Ⓑ Ⓒ Ⓓ
16 Ⓐ Ⓑ Ⓒ Ⓓ
17 Ⓐ Ⓑ Ⓒ Ⓓ
18 Ⓐ Ⓑ Ⓒ Ⓓ
19 Ⓐ Ⓑ Ⓒ Ⓓ
20 Ⓐ Ⓑ Ⓒ Ⓓ

Directions for marking answers

- Use a No. 2 pencil. Do NOT use ink.
- Make dark marks and bubble in your answers completely.
- If you change an answer, erase your first mark completely.

Right
Ⓐ ● Ⓒ Ⓓ

Wrong
Ⓐ ⊗ Ⓒ Ⓓ
Ⓐ Ⓑ Ⓒ Ⓓ

③ **STUDENT IDENTIFICATION**

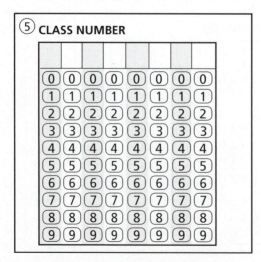

Is this your Social Security number?
Yes ☐ No ☐

④ **TEST DATE**

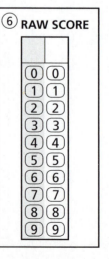

⑤ **CLASS NUMBER**

⑥ **RAW SCORE**